Of, By and For the People

from the perspective of an Earth Human Being

by

Angelo Patrick Arteman

Of, By and For the People

Of, By and For the People

from the perspective of
an Earth Human Being

by

Angelo Patrick Arteman

January 2014

This work is intended for the benefit of the Peoples of Earth.
It may be copied, shared and distributed freely as long as it remains unaltered but not sold. It may be translated into any language as long as the original English is also in the same document for readers to verify the authenticity of the translation. It may be published with commentary as long as the original text is kept intact and the commentary portion is clearly distinguished as such.

Information *wants* to be free. An idea cannot be owned as it exists apart from any one being, in the mental plane where it can be viewed by those who learn to see. Share with others, that which is given freely to you.

Dedication

This work is dedicated to my children and the youth of this planet, that they may know peace, justice and freedom from oppression in their lifetimes. And to the People who have shown light into the dark corners, some who died in the process, that others may learn the truth. And to those individuals who have helped me in this life, without whom I could not have written this book.

First Edition, Revision One
21 January, 2014

Preface

I was born on August 30, 1961 at about 1:26 in the afternoon in Peoria, Illinois. In the heart of the Shield of the United States of America, which is what I fancy Illinois looks like on a map. It was a not a pretty birth. My mother suffered in a most painful way. The cold handed doctor all but killed me in the process. Maybe because, according to the way of thinking of the doctor working for the Roman Catholic hospital, I was just a second class citizen. A child born with extra Original Sin. My birth mother was sent away to have me in shame. I was taken away at birth. We did not meet again for 25 years.

The doctor used some kind of tool that crushed my head and popped a blood vessel deep in my right brain. I was born crippled. A cerebral palsy child. I can say, and this is how it feels, that I was touched by a finger from the hand of Death deep inside my brain at birth. Death would be a close companion throughout my life. This may seem unbelievable to some of you, but part of myself has always been in the realm of the dead.

Par for the course when you are born in sin I guess. By the way, what kind of idiocy is it to believe in "Original Sin"? There is really not much more of a dehumanizing concept than that. I never thought it made much sense and never accepted it. But millions are fooled into believing such crap. Not to judge too harshly, but it is our duty to question the bullshit and not accept it.

So, the left side of my body would spasm uncontrollably. What was to become of me? I remember laying in what I know now was a crib with wooden slats, on a terrazzo floor, in a big cold room with a high ceiling. Of course everything is big when seen through the eyes of a baby. Several orbs of light were above me, in a circle. They were beings of light. They discussed what to do amongst themselves. Was I to stay or abandon this broken vessel? The message I got was they were going to "re-wire" and repair my brain.

So I was to stay in this damaged vehicle and attempt to fulfill my mission in this world. Of course, not too clear on what that mission was. Sometimes I think I was thrown into this situation at this time, on this planet just cause someone wanted to see what would happen. Who knows? Maybe that is why all of us are here?

I was eventually taken in by a family in Illinois. After a time, when it turned out the repairs that no one on this Earth knew about but me, worked, they decided to keep me. I became the ninth child in a family of ten children. My name was changed and a "sanitized" birth certificate was made.

Mom & Dad wanted a big Catholic family. They were certainly dedicated. They had endured their own hardships in life. It is not for me to judge them. I certainly would have been worse off if they had not taken me in.

When ideas are presented, does it really matter who writes or speaks that idea? No, damn it, it does not. What matters is the idea, or the song, the art, that which

2

is created. If we were to judge the works of our species by judging who made these works, how much good art would remain?

This is not about me. This is about You. All of You who are Humans on this planet called Earth, having an experience. Those of you who are spiritually and mentally immortal, but temporarily inhabiting a physical body, an awareness of this existence. That is a big distinction, because not everyone you see is Human or born here. And where a person's immortal spirit comes from is more significant than the history of the body they are in.

It is important to understand, there are many, many different peoples on, in and around this planet. This book is intended for those who are good at heart; who love the Human species and are willing to demand their rights; and are willing to break free from the many oppressors who lay in wait, even before birth, to enslave us.

If any of you need to be controlled or need to surrender to some entity who wants your sacrifice and subservience, get away from me. This book is not for you. Maybe someday when you are ready it will be.

If you feel that my choice of words is vulgar or obscene, I would like to educate you on what is really vulgar and obscene. The subjugation, manipulation and attempted control of others is the real vulgar obscenity. War, injustice, oppression, inequitable distribution of food and wealth, GMO being substituted for food, chimeras, too much secrecy, child sacrifice, blood sacrifice of any kind, torture. Need I go on?

Of, By and For the People

I cannot write this without expressing my outrage and anger over what I see is going on. That I have managed to calm down enough to write at all has taken many years. If you can do better, please do. For me, this is the best I can do. And I am not sorry if it disappoints or bothers anyone. Not going to apologize for this. Well, maybe, after all of the oppressors of my People stop their atrocities and apologize, I could reconsider.

In this edition, I have toned it down quite a bit. Felt it necessary to remove some of what most people would consider coarse language. It was difficult as the F word is the most versatile word in the English language. This is an emotional work for me. Really poured my heart out like never before. Still, I may reach a wider audience this way. My gut tells me the same people who could not handle the earlier drafts will not be able to handle the truth no mater how it is conveyed. They might be more inclined to at least read it this way though, might sink in later.

What I have learned is not easily provable. Some of what I know is from what other people would call subjective reality. We all have senses and perceptions beyond what is called the physical world. I certainly do anyway.

I am expressing my own personal beliefs and ideas, to share with you. I know that no matter what I say or write, no truth is ever conveyed to anyone who does not have the energy to receive it.

My intent is not to write a scholarly work with detailed citations and references. I really do not have the patience and probably even the skill for that. Also, many times in my life I have had discussions with others, where I express my subjective observations. Many times, the other person has said I must have read this or that or seen this or that documentary, speaker or other source. When in truth, I had not seen, read or heard the source they refer to. They act confused sometimes, as if it were not possible for a person to have their own analysis.

So many people seem to have to be told by a so called authority to believe anything. I would be dead a long time ago if that were true in my life. It is a bit like saying people have visited from other planets, times or dimensions only if their political or religious "leaders" were to say so. It does not matter to them that they have their own awareness. Or that thousands of people have come forward with disclosure, for instance. Or that they have been lied to by these same "leaders" as a matter of course. Guess it is just a part of human nature.

This book provides a positive goal for Humans Being on this planet, who are facing an existential threat to their existence, to begin to focus upon. That is all of us. It is not enough to turn away from the old, failed order. It takes a positive, objective goal to be established for it to be manifest into reality by our collective intent.

Bottom line, I am writing this so I can rest more comfortably. If somehow this leads to a more peaceful and just organization of the Humans Being, then I be trippin happily on my way, passing through this world and back through the veil.

Prolog

With this book, I am trying to convey what are essentially subjective thoughts and beliefs. A person's beliefs make up their paradigm of reality. But it is unlikely any two persons have the same paradigm of reality. So don't get too bent out of shape if you do not agree. If you find my observations and suggestions useful, and I hope you do, it is enough. But please do not get caught up in the minutia.

I could provide names of people who I believe have presented very great material, who are actual scholars. There are some listed in the Bibliography. But there is no one source that I completely agree with or that has all the pieces. There are many pieces to this puzzle. And what is right for one person might not be the best for another person.

Any real solution has to not care so much about our differences but about our similarities.

I am like you, because I am not like you. We are unique, all of us. Everyone has their unique perspective in time and space. I fully realize no two persons see, hear or otherwise sense exactly the same. Some to a larger degree of difference than others. This is important to keep in mind, in order to begin to understand each other.

This is my attempt to contribute solutions to the existential threat we face as a species, as a People. We need some form of organization to defend ourselves from our declared and undeclared enemies. But if we create an authoritarian style organization, then what is there worth defending?

It is my experience that government can be and often is the most vile, deceitful, dishonest, corrupt and disgusting institution there is. All governments are corrupt or unjust. I am not aware of anywhere on this world where this is not the case. The only possible exceptions are short lived. A good social order must prevent oppressive, authoritarian government from existing in our lives.

I respect no centrally organized religion. This is distinct from a philosophy, belief or code of conduct. Centrally organized religion is a major source of strife, injustice, war, poverty, mind control and oppression. If that statement pisses you off, well you most likely deserve it. How about you question the bullshit and free your mind?

I do totally understand that many good or well intended people are in these middle eastern religions and their spinoffs. That is the Catholic Church, other variations on Christian Churches, Islam, Judaism, Luciferianism and the Church of Satan. These are ultimately a form of slavery. You have better already inside you. You are directly a part of the real Creator. There is no limit to your Consciousness. Now is not the time to continue on as you have. Free your mind and soul for yourself. But some will not find that to be enough motivation. You have a duty to free your mind and soul for the benefit of all Humans Being.

We are being enslaved at an extremely rapid rate. These organizations are actively involved in this process though most of their members do not know it. All it takes is the collective will and intent of the People for that to stop. Liberation comes one Person at a time.

I actually have met the Master called Jesus or Sananda. He is real. There is no major Christian church that teaches what He taught. He taught me more in five minutes than I have learned in the whole rest of my life. That is Real. That is direct. Aum.

All of these organization have positive teachings. Rat poison is 99% good healthy food and 1% Sodium Fluoride.

I believe that most people, souls, incarnating on this planet are linked to three or four interstellar races. And that we are genetically related to very many interstellar species. Some among Pleiadians are said to have a saying: "Politics *is* Religion" according to Alex Collier in "Defending Sacred Ground". I agree. So this is my political statement to all. My personal religion. I do not need converts. I do not need others to agree for me to feel right about this.

All of you are created by the infinite source of all creation. You and I are a part of the consciousness of the creator. Even though our physical body has been genetically engineered, those beings who did this are not our creator. They sure want me and you to be their slaves and play god to us though. Our spirit and mind bodies exist far beyond the confines of this temporal existence, and theirs as well.

Of, By and For the People

There is no need for an intermediary. No need to prostrate yourself or surrender your will to some wanna be controlling entity who seeks your subservience. I believe it is actually a kind of treason to ourselves and to the real Creator to do this.

The source of all creation has made us co-creators, however small a part of this vast, possibly infinite universe. Though I am just another one of billions, that does not lessen my status as a sovereign being with rights. Rights that I do demand for myself and yourself.

This book is about law. Law is a living concept. People do not exist to serve law. Legitimate law exists only to serve the People.

We are at war for our survival. This planet is a battleground of cosmic proportions. I do not trust any entity from anywhere without merit. As Humans Being, a good social order is extremely critical to adopt to gain the unity to defend ourselves from both malevolent and well intended beings who seek to exterminate or dominate and control the Humans on this planet and elsewhere.

The way this works is relatively simple. As co-creators with free will, each of us manifest reality through our intent. When that intent is synchronized to the relatively same goal, that future gets created. The game of the malevolent beings, always it seems, is to get us to create our own dystopian future. That is what the apocalyptic religious teachings are all about. Who do you think created that? Not our Creator, I can assure you.

There are classes of beings which literally feed on our fear and negative emotions. They can been seen by psychics hovering over battlefields for instance. But, did you know movie theaters too? Horror movies create fear which they feed on. They are parasitic because they cannot create for themselves. Fear lowers our vibrational frequency. The object is to increase our vibrational frequency. Love is the highest frequency.

It is in this context this book is written. I am proposing a more utopian future for us to manifest into being. True Utopia is unobtainable by definition. I want to move in that direction for a change and have a good time on the way.

Chapter 1

History Influencing this Book

When the united States was formed, the King of England at the time, signed the Treaty of Paris granting his Sovereignty, as a King to the Colonies and its Citizens. This is kind of important in that no such thing had happened before or since, at least from the last time humans were all but made extinct (again), about 12,500 years ago.

What I believe it really meant was, "If I grant sovereignty, you will never organize or unite and will be easily re-taken over and enslaved as subjects again." But for the example of the Algonquin Nation and their consultation to the Continental Congress, a republic of sovereign individuals may not have happened.

A read of the Constitution of the united States presents one with obvious injustice and other problems:

Slavery, WHAT? NO! People are NOT property!

Women were not allowed to vote or have equal legal status? What? Not acceptable.

You have to own land and be of a certain parentage to be a citizen? Does not sound right to me. Does not pass the sniff test.

So the original Constitution was a big deal, an improvement, but not good enough to create a good or sustainable society which preserves our Rights.

Of, By and For the People

The men representing the colonies would not accept the Constitution without clearly defined restrictions on government. The Bill of Rights was created and approved.

Even though the Bill of Rights has never been actually enforced or fully implemented, that document stands as the highest achievement so far. Even though these Rights no longer exist as you and I no longer live under the rule of law, they represent a pretty solid Declaration of Rights. So, We the People must have a clear and simple Declaration of Rights. Something to reference for ourselves and to show others.

The example of a republic of sovereign individuals with declared and established In-alienable Rights bestowed by the Creator is a good one. What I endeavor to do is build on that example. Improve on it.

Let us examine the Declaration of Independence drafted by Thomas Jefferson.

The context is clear. The motivations spelled out. But it is still a reactive document. Much of the text does not really apply in the context of today. But, one line stands alone, above and beyond all else. It is true and cherished deep in my heart:

"We hold these truths to be self-evident, that all men are created equal, that they are endowed by their Creator with certain unalienable Rights, that among these are Life, Liberty and the pursuit of Happiness."

Wow! I need to pause to shed a tear. I cry happily for the beauty of that statement and for the courage of the people who signed it. I cry sadly for the fact that it took 10,000 years, figuratively, for it to happen. I cry that nowhere on the planet is there a government that does not violate it.

The Declaration of Independence goes on:

"That to secure these rights, Governments are instituted among Men, deriving their just powers from the consent of the governed, --That whenever any Form of Government becomes destructive of these ends, it is the Right of the People to alter or to abolish it, and to institute new Government, laying its foundation on such principles and organizing its powers in such form, as to them shall seem most likely to effect their Safety and Happiness. Prudence, indeed, will dictate that Governments long established should not be changed for light and transient causes; and accordingly all experience hath shewn, that mankind are more disposed to suffer, while evils are sufferable, than to right themselves by abolishing the forms to which they are accustomed. But when a long train of abuses and usurpations, pursuing invariably the same Object evinces a design to reduce them under absolute Despotism, it is their right, it is their duty, to throw off such Government, and to provide new Guards for their future security."

Pretty ballsy statement and correct. The use of the word men is an issue I have a problem with though. It really was a government instituted by men and not men and women. What is up with that? I want more than just another form of repression and control to replace an older one. If you can get half the population to dominate and effectively oppress the other half, the divide and conquer method is well on its way. There is also no clear reference to the Rights of Children.

While it is easy to agree with the need to throw-off oppression, the newly formed government was quickly corrupted.

I cite the Whiskey Rebellion which was put down by murder. George Washington just happened to be the wealthiest man in America and held the largest estate. But, more significantly, he owned the largest whiskey distillery in America. So, he enforced a tax against the consent of the governed. A tax that had to be paid in cash, which the mountain folk, with their simple home stills, subsistence living and cashless economy did not have. Did not matter to him or the murder for hire thugs that attacked the People, that it was clearly a conflict of interest and a plain violation of basic Rights.

If you want to know more, I suggest reading the late Howard Zinn's "A People's History of the United States." A real eye opener that.

The united States was fully destroyed back in the 1860's by the Jesuits and their mind controlled and manipulated minions. If you do not know that, I suggest you learn. You will not learn the truth in school. You will not learn the truth in any approved text book. I cannot prove it to you. The truth is there for you to find it.

Since that time, there have been several Coup d'états in the United States. One happened in 1913, one in 1935, in 1947, 1963, 1968, and 2000. I am sure others can point out more, these are of particular significance to me.

1865 - War between the States. Ended with the destruction and enslavement of the Southern States and then everyone in the new authoritarian state. The original 13th Amendment was quietly no longer printed and hidden with a new 13th amendment which was never legally ratified. A 14th amendment, also not ratified by law, which declared everyone subjects of a corporation called the United States. The legal system was obliterated and replaced by the British Accredited Registry Association. This was the sort of thing forbidden by the original 13th Amendment.

The American Army was the most technologically advanced in the world by the end of the war. That Army was turned on the Native Peoples of North America. Some of the worst genocide and atrocities ever committed were made to happen. Personally, that crime is so horribly bad, it is reason enough to walk away from all that and start anew, as I am proposing in this book. This time we will be taught by the surviving wise men and women of these ancient and spiritual cultures.

1913 - The Federal Reserve Act was illegally put in place after many key people were murdered, bribed, blackmailed and threatened. With this act, Congress abdicated its duty and responsibility, effectively committing high treason against the People. This act subjected the People to economic control by the criminal, reptilian banking cabal based in The City, in London, which in turn is an agent of the Vatican.

Of, By and For the People

All roads lead to Rome. According to the researcher and author Jordan Maxwell, the Roman Catholic Church is over 3,500 years old. Lots of time. If they were for world peace and legitimate government Of, By and For the People, I think it would be in evidence by now. It is fair to say they have had their chance and failed.

1935 – Some judges of the court system decided that the government had effectively been bankrupted by the global banking cabal. They decided that from now on, everyone had given their implied consent to all repugnant law (laws that exceed power granted to government in the Bill of Rights or are otherwise in violation of the original Constitution). Rulings by judges now became precedents, another completely unconstitutional practice in which judges effectively dictated legislation. States began to license basic rights. License means privilege to do that which is otherwise illegal.

This included such things as marriage, which was a double illegal act in that the Bill of Rights expressly prohibited government from enacting any law regarding the establishment of religion. So all you who think it is so important to get big oppressor's permission to marry as you see fit, you have been fooled at least two levels deep. You already have that right. It is an In-alienable Right. These rights cannot be granted by anyone but the Creator. None but the Creator can take these Rights away.

1947 - The creation of the Orwellian named National Security Act was a clear violation of the Rights of the People. It effectively convinced many that a Secret Government no longer had to inform the People of their criminal acts, even when directed against the People. Actual National Security has only one legitimate objective, to preserve the Rights of the People and ensure they are protected.

1963 - After the mafioso Joe Kennedy had a stroke, young Jack and Bobby decided to do good with their power. While not all was good, they made a major attempt to restore the Republic. As we know now, GHW Bush, J. Edgar Hoover, Lyndon Johnson, the Joint Chiefs of Staff, the Federal Reserve Board, the CIA, Richard Nixon, the Secret Service, the Banking Cabal, the Vatican and other elements of organized crime and media conglomerates assassinated and/or covered-up the assassination of President Kennedy. As part of their operation, they made sure of the timing, in broad daylight, on national television. They made sure of the location, the 33 degree latitude. I guess they just wanted to prove that evil, criminal forces rule this former constitutional republic. Over 50 material witnesses were murdered over the ensuing two weeks. The criminals were quite successful.

There is a plethora of well documented research to support this. But all you have to do is see that there was an explosion and fire in the John F. Kennedy Presidential Library on April 15, 2013, the week more information was to be made available to the People. What specifically was destroyed or removed? And the fact that the "official" records were sealed, that is concealed, from the People for 50 years. Then that time was extended to prove the criminal cabal still runs the alleged federal government.

Of, By and For the People

An aspect of the significance of the assassination of JFK which has been hidden deeply, is the fact that an ancient city, 420,000 years old was found buried near Dallas in a county named after the find, Rock Wall, Texas. It held a repository of high technology developed by ancient space/time travelers. Josh Reeves has done great work in researching and presenting this. He created two hardcore documentaries on the subject in his "Lost Secrets of Ancient America Volumes I & II". This information apparently would have been made pubic in the speech about to be given to the People. This trove was discovered in the 1800's!!!

This suppression of information and technology, especially energy and medical technology, is essential to subjugate, manipulate and oppress the People.

1968 - Bobby Kennedy had just won the California Primary and for all practical purposes was the de-facto president elect. So a criminal element within ITT Security was contracted to shoot Bobby in the back of the head in front of his ardent supporters. A nation mourned. Bobby was not all good. Who among us is? But, he wanted to right many wrongs, restore a Constitutional Republic and bring peace and prosperity to the People. He also backed a lost concept in this country - Justice.

I do not even want to get into what happened to the Carter family after that honest man was elected president. What I have been told... Someday that truth will come out.

Some of you may wonder why I am not pointing out the attempted assassination of President Ronald Reagan. Ronald Reagan was forced to accept GHW Bush as his running mate. This proved almost fatal. See, back then was the early days of CNN. When this mouthpiece of the global criminal cabal was still in its infancy, it had a policy of allowing unedited news reports to be broadcast. This created excitement, trust and viewership. As it should.

On March 30, 1981, there was a live interview of the doctor who lead the operation to save President Reagan. I just happened to see this myself. The doctor announced that he removed a thin disk the size of a dime, with razor sharp edges. He said it had slipped between his ribs and nearly sliced through his aorta. (That is the big artery leading away from the heart) He said because it missed, President Reagan would be fine and recover soon. I think he said something like it missed by a quarter inch, but if it struck his aorta, President Reagan would have died.

Hmmm. Lets see, Reagan has just made correct and disparaging remarks about the Federal Reserve Bank two weeks earlier. He suggested abolishing the income tax as well. Vice President Bush just happened to have lunch with John Hinkley Jr. the day before the attempted assassination. Mr. Hinkley had a regular gun. A .38 calliber if I remember correctly. He did not hit the President, who had just won the election in the greatest landslide in history. So who did? Oh, the Secret Service agent next to the president.

Reagan was only on the ticket in the first place because he managed to cover up key evidence in the Bobby Kennedy assassination investigation in California. But after this happened Mr. Bush ran the show. Lets see, from then until today.... Yup, nothing new. Same old same old. So that is why it is not on my list of Coup d'états affecting this book.

2000 - The election was extremely fraudulent resulting in a smirking chimp pretending to be president and the undermining of the last vestiges of what at one time was representative government. Of course the cabal behind this regime attacked New York in the now infamous psychological operation against the American people. The result is the establishment of the Fourth Reich with all the fixings.

The NAZI's never surrendered. Some escaped to various locations in South America and Antarctica. Some were brought to the United States and Russia where they assumed positions of power in the government. This is more true of the United States. Nazism actually began in the United States, there was already a base of support. I could not get a handle on global politics without this fundamental understanding.

The next step involves something called Exo-Politics. That is taking into account various species, I will call them civilizations, which are not Humans Being. The humanoid form is apparently not unusual though, so some look like us or we look like them. It is not correct to say extra-terrestrial life, as some of these entities have lived or do live on this planet as well. Some just come and go. Some are inter-dimensional beings. Some are time travelers. All major governments are aware of this and have dealings with various groups.

At this time, the former united States is under Zionist-NAZI nuclear blackmail and enslavement. I call them Zio-nazis for short since it is much the same people. It sickens me to no end. But what sickens me even more is the mindless automatons who accept this or support it or are in denial about it.

I am NOT OK with this situation.

This is NOT ACCEPTABLE!!

So, we do not have a legitimate government and the failed state is hopelessly beyond repair. What is worse, these enemies of all free souls are actively at war with the People of Earth. You and I are under attack.

The good news is the powers that wanna be are a bit dull, as all creativity and real intelligence is suppressed. Well some are pretty smart and have serious psychic powers, but they just do not get it. This is why they use Humans Being to create for them and then wipe their memory or monitor inventive minds to steal their ideas. This is also has a lot to do the ridiculous secrecy contracts that hide so much. As a result, their structurally unsustainable system is collapsing. Even as they tighten their grip, their fist holds less and less.

Chapter 2

Freedom, Sovereignty & Discussion of Rights

What is the best organizational structure for a group of free and sovereign individuals. As humans being, it is actually not possible to survive for very long without some degree of cooperation. Not just us, but all mammals have some degree of interdependence in order for the species to survive.

What is Freedom? What is Sovereignty? These questions are deeply personal. Only an individual can answer these for themselves. And, if you are like me, that answer can change over time as I experience and learn in the course of living.

Personal freedom and sovereignty suggest independence and autonomy. But we are inherently social animals. (party animals too) No matter how advanced an individual becomes, when in a group, rules of behavior will always apply. Personal boundaries and mutual respect are critical to peace between individuals.

The concept of democracy is basically one person, one vote and all group decisions must be voted on. In practicality, this never works except on a small scale with like minded individuals. It quickly becomes mob or majority rule with oppression or death to the minority.

Of, By and For the People

When you hear a politician talk about democracy, they are just lying deceivers. They are confident the majority will be effectively manipulated to oppress the minority on any given issue.

Democracy will always fail except on a small scale. In a democracy, you have no rights that can be enforced except through force. The united States was created to prevent a democracy from happening. Democracy was probably the greatest fear the framers of the Constitution had. This is not blasphemy. This is truth.

Not everyone has the time, inherent skills or even interest to be informed on all matters. People have many, many skill sets and talents. But no one person has them all. Even if everyone has the same information, the levels of understanding of a particular subject can be quite different. And everyone has a life cycle to deal with. Our capabilities vary throughout our lives as we grow and age.

What is the value of an uninformed vote? It is potentially destructive. Those who are more informed will be appalled when over ruled by those who are not. This results, for practical reasons, in a separation or breakdown of the community. Which defeats the whole purpose and leads to community decay and eventually death.

The solution that evolved is a representative republic where each individual remains sovereign. Individuals are selected and elected to a group whose job it is to be informed of the issues. The idea is to have better decision making for the whole society. This should result in a stronger community where the members and the society are more likely to survive. If the representative body fails in its duty to represent the people and uphold their Rights, it will face the will of the masses sooner or later anyway. And it could get ugly.

These questions are important. I know of no so called government on this planet, at this time, which allows freedom or sovereignty. No one will give these to you or me. I and you have to make that happen in our own lives by thinking and doing, by being free and sovereign.

I want to create a new and better society out of the ashes. One that does not necessarily war with the old order, but can act as a galvanizing and sustaining force to unite and free the Peoples of Earth. A social order that can be duplicated, without strong central authority, in any community, by anyone. In short, a blueprint that can go viral and begin to improve living conditions for everyone. A system that is in harmony with Earth and Sol and the natural order of life.

This community / society needs a short, correct name. One which is not loaded with too much baggage and has global appeal. What do you suggest? No 'ists or 'isms please and not New World Order as the lips which have spoken that term defile it.

A strong Declaration of Rights is essential to counter balance the power of a group over an individual.

When it comes to basic matters, where you do not have to be an expert to understand the issue, the democratic principle where everyone votes does apply. For instance, a group is elected which can then distill a decision and present it to all the people to vote on.

When a representative body needs a decision implemented, it is sometimes essential or even critical to build consensus in the community first. This is human nature, in my opinion, and not likely to change anytime soon. Even when it is critical to the survival of the society, people do not like other person's decisions forced on them. By gaining acceptance and building consensus first, everyone becomes a willing participant. This can lead to a more smooth and efficient process of implementation.

I would argue that major decisions affecting the whole community would need to be put to a vote of the people in order to prevent abuse of power by the representative group.

But I am trying to define an organizational structure which can apply locally and globally. The need is for effective communication and coordinated action. Information needs to be shared. Communication is the key. The free flow of information cannot be allow to be restricted.

What does not exist, at least in the States, is a true public forum for debate. A public space is necessary for a community or society to function effectively.

We live in a time where there does not exist a Free Press. The Zio-Nazis have made a big deal over the consolidation of media. In the US, estimates are that 97% of all newspapers, publishing houses, radio stations, television stations, movie theaters, movie production studios, and music publishing are owned or controlled by six conglomerates.

Of, By and For the People

This is a false front. In reality, there is only one mega-conglomerate. This is because of inter-locking director-ships on each of these mega barf conglomerate's Board of Directors. While I am referring to the US here, it is my understanding that this pattern continues world wide. These controllers are certainly not loyal to any nation and are enemies of the People.

Maybe government is not the answer. Maybe it is not even necessary at all. I wish.

The reality is we are under attack and still face an existential threat to our existence individually and as a species. Like a chess game, there are some moves one might like to make, but the immediate threat must be dealt with first.

We must find a way to organize for our mutual defense. A by product is that it should lead to a much higher standard of living than any of us have known before in this world. United we are strong. Divided, we fall. We are in free fall right now if anyone is paying attention.

What is necessary is a form of dispute resolution that is fair and equitable.

When rights are declared, many laws do not need to be written. I and you are free to act in Life, Liberty and the Pursuit of Happiness, until it violates those very rights of another. It is really that simple. Environmental pollution, for example is not illegal due to some law, but it is a violation of the rights of others. It needs to be resolved in that context.

Age is a factor. A child needs to be protected from harm and have Rights, but should not be held accountable to the same degree as an adult.

At what age is a person an adult member of society? Some would argue that no person should serve in the military defense of society without full rights as an adult. This is basically about physical maturity. What about mental maturity? Not everyone reaches physical or mental maturity at the same age in their lives. Who would determine when mental maturity is reached?

I propose full adult rights begin when a person has completed 17 years. This is a compromise. Some young people will reach physical maturity at and earlier or later age. It is important that a standard be fairly applied to all.

The whole issue of mental maturity is too subjective. Next thing we know, everyone has to pass some form of politicized test to vote. This is not acceptable. If, someday well into the future a mutually agreed upon objective criteria can be set, then this issue can be addressed again. Otherwise, just pick the age of eighteen, which is the completion of 17 years.

In dealing with the Rights of Children, it is a balance between the Rights of a Parent and the Rights of a child. Where the family structure is intact, the community should not be allowed to interfere. But if a child is in an abusive environment, they need to be able to seek help outside that environment.

When a child does seek help or another adult is aware of a situation where a child would and should seek help but is prevented, at what point is an intervention necessary? In almost all cases, taking the child from their family is more destructive then the situation they are in already. Who would have the authority to do so anyway? If they have temporary access to a safe haven, that could ease the stress. Any intervention must be done with the purpose of healing the situation.

One extreme, is the parent has full life and death authority over their children. The other extreme is when a child has a small bruise from playing and is trying to manipulate their parents or accuses them falsely. The first case is too barbaric and provides no protection of the Child's Rights. The second case could lead to the destruction of a family, and the violation of the Parent's Rights and result in real harm to the life of the child, if there is an intervention.

If a person wants to have a healthy part of their body cut off, they must make that decision when they are an adult. Parents have no right to inflict such barbaric acts upon their children as sexual mutilation. Anyone who does this to a child and any parent that authorizes it would be held accountable for a criminal act. That does not mean breaking up the family or necessarily jail time for the first offense. The person actually committing this crime should be dealt with severely. This has to stop.

If a parent is determined to have a pattern of violating the rights of a their child or children, or commit serious injury, then yes, a warrant should be issued and they would face a court for their actions and could result in jail time.

I propose that each group of 20,000 people or less appoint a small council of elders which only address these family situations. They would maintain a safe haven for the child to go to temporarily in an emergency. The council would operate with the goal of healing the problem and restoring the family unit.

Chapter 3

Rights of the People

It is in this context that I suggest the following Rights. The order they are presented is not so important. What is important is the acceptance and actualization of all of them in our personal lives. These Rights determine our relationship with each other. With Rights comes Responsibility.

It is very important that the Rights, once accepted by an individual, are applied to all People without regard to their ethnicity, gender, age or location. In other words, a person cannot expect to have Rights for themselves that they would deny to another. If I have Rights, and I do, then you have those Rights. It cannot be any other way.

Individuals who join me in consenting to the Rights of the People may be called Citizens of this yet to be named Global Community / Society.

Here is my list of Rights for all Humans Being on this planet.

The word People is meant to represent all gender and ethnicity. Person is singular for People. Representative Group or Groups refers to members of this Society. Community refers to living centers of members of this Society.

===

Of, By and For the People

01: Each individual is unique and has a unique relationship with their Creator. Therefore the People have a Right to their own beliefs, thoughts emotions and free expression thereof, including in the Public Space.

02: People have the Right to adorn, dress or not and present themselves as they see fit.

03: People retain the Right to their body and therefore control of the consumption and use of foods and medicines. This includes the right to be free of forced medication, implantation, injection, medical procedure, poison or otherwise be harmed. Children and babies have the Right to not be sexually mutilated.

04: A pregnant woman has the right to determine the course of her own pregnancy.

05: People have the right to choose their final exit from the physical body as they deem appropriate.

06: As Humans, we have a symbiotic relationship with the cannabis plant. No person has the right to tax or deny the use and cultivation of this most important plant. The only known plant which by itself can sustain Human life and civilization.

07: People have the right to freedom of speech through voice, song, writing or other art of self expression. However, a Person can be held accountable if their speech or self expression results in *directly* causing physical harm or violates the Rights of another person.

08: People have the Right to peaceably assemble without restriction.

09:    People have the Right to be free of harmful substances added to food, water, air and soil and other environmental pollution.

10:    People have the Right to a healthy and safe living,
working and playing environment. But they also have a
Right to take risks upon themselves, for one example
sporting activities which can never be totally free of danger or potential harm.

11:    People have the Right to full disclosure of information from any organization they participate in or organizational body created to meet the needs of a community.

12:    People have the right to access any data or information collected or stored regarding themselves by any person, group or organization.   This includes the right to
challenge, amend and/or correct such information.

13:    People have the right to be secure in their person,
home, papers, thoughts, digital media, effects and private
communications, against unreasonable search and/or
seizure.

14:    People have a Right to self defense and to defend
others if necessary.   Therefore People have the right to
keep and bear arms and learn martial arts. This is does
not include the use of excessive force. Weapons of mass
destruction, however, need to be under secure military
control.

15:    People have the Right to contract freely with others
as long as the enforcement of that contract or agreement
does not result in harm to the individual. Therefore, Peo-

ple have the Right to terminate their consent to a contract or agreement. If a contract results in harm, or is expected to harm the individual, that agreement may be invalidated immediately.

16:   People have a Right to access and/or use Public Space. For example, a public space, like a park, cannot be closed during certain times, for the purpose of restricting access or open to some People, but not others.

17:   A duly appointed body created by community consensus may have only the powers specifically granted to it.   No group or organization may be granted powers which result in the violation of the Rights of the People.

18:   If any Citizen shall accept, claim, receive, or retain any title of nobility or honor, or accept and retain any present, pension, office, or emolument of any kind whatever, from any emperor, king, prince, or foreign power, such person shall cease to be a Citizen of this Society, and shall be incapable of holding any office of trust or profit within this Society.

19:   People have the right to be quiet and to not accuse themselves. This means forced confession and attempted forced confession is expressly forbidden.

20:   People cannot be property. Involuntary servitude, including taxation of labor or services rendered is expressly prohibited.

21:   A group or organization of people is not a person and cannot have legal standing as an actual person.

22:    No single law created by any elected legislature can be too long or complex. If it takes more than 20 minutes for an average person to read and/or is not in clear, straight, understandable language, that law is null and void.

23:    Any elected person who votes to pass any law which is deemed to violate this Bill of Rights is subject to recall and a new election held for their office or seat in the group as soon as is practical.

24:    A mother and father will have joint custody of their children, even in a break-up, unless they agree to another arrangement between themselves or through a mediator.

25:    A Person shall be free from double jeopardy. That is we cannot be accused and a hearing held more than once for the same offense. A single act cannot result in multiple charges. One charge has to be chosen.

26:    A Person has the Right to Travel as is practical. Public roads and public forms of transportation must be available to all.

27:    A Person has the Right to be accused and brought to trial only for acts which violate the Rights of another Person. There has to be an actual injured party. Entrapment and Sting Operations are crimes in and of themselves and the injured party is their target.

28:    No law or treaty can be valid which has not been made public and read aloud at least three times, and these public readings spaced apart in time at least one day, before being voted for approval. Truthful authorship of any pending law or treaty has to be made public before any vote for approval can take place.

29:    No treaty or binding agreement can be made by any representative person or group in the name of this Society which violates these Rights. Any treaties or binding agreements made with a party outside this Society must be made public and is subject to a vote for approval by the entire global community with a two thirds majority before it can take effect.

30:    This defining of certain rights, shall not be construed to deny or disparage others retained by the People.

Chapter 4

Role of the Community / Society

I present two entwined questions, the answers to them define our relationship to each other:

What is the responsibility of a community to its members?

What is the responsibility of a member to the community?

My answer to that question may be a bit unorthodox, but please bear with me on this. I present this example for argument sake only.

= =

I am a King of an ancient tradition. In this role every morning I sense the mood of my People. As Sol (our Sun) rises over the land and sea, the clean rivers and streams run through towns and fields. My People are stirring in their homes. I can hear the cries and laughter of children. Fishermen have set out to sea, some are returning with their catch. Farmers begin tending their fields. Merchants set up their shops. Blacksmiths are getting their fires started. Bakers begin their days production. My Army, always vigilant, guards and protects the realm. My Navy patrols the harbors and ensures freedom of the sea from pirates and raiders.

Of, By and For the People

There are no prisoners. Serious transgressors are executed and minor transgressors do not deserve prison. There is almost no crime.

This day, is a good day. My people are happy. That makes me feel a bit more at peace. Peace pervades the land. My people are reasonably safe and secure.

The simple laws of the land are carved into stone pillars for all to see. They do not change with the whim of the King. I am as bound by them as everyone else. If I transgress, the People will know and I can no longer effectively rule.

I have been taught from early youth to love my People with all my heart and serve them with all my ability. It is my duty to ensure no one goes hungry. To secure their safety and well being. It is my duty to collect the greater portion of all food produced. The food is brought into community storage to protect from famine and spoilage. Anyone of the Realm can come to the castle to dine at every meal prepared twice daily. They can come to pick up food to take home. That is what it is there for.

The healers serve everyone equally. All arms produced are for the realm. The wealth of the kingdom belongs to the People. The sign of Peace is the sharing of water.

= =

I actually have memories of this time from an incarnation over 2300 years ago, but that is besides the point. Some of you might think me crazy for even saying these things. I get that a lot, oh well.

Of, By and For the People

In this model, the government exists to serve and protect the People. And the People serve the Realm. But what could possibly go wrong? I think we all know. Hint: it did not end well and certainly did not last unto the present time.

OK, something messed up happened. Those great and powerful laws written in stone were applied. Someone was executed who was loved by the People and did not deserve it, except under the law. The whole thing fell apart. I can never express how much I regret this. If there is anything I have learned it is what was stated before, "People do not exist to serve the Law, Legitimate Law exists to serve the People." Just because it is written or carved into stone that is not enough. I wish I had died instead of her or prevented it from happening. Life is more valuable and more important than strict application of law. Sometimes the strict application of law is an injustice. Sometimes injustice can have severe consequences.

Therefore this model is just not sustainable or acceptable with self aware Humans Being. Good People will demand more. I demand more. We are creatures of emotion. Too much power vested in anyone is a recipe for failure. This can happen for many reasons, even reasons beyond the person playing the role. The role with too much power becomes the object of intrigue and is coveted by individuals who by nature would be even less likely to handle the role to the benefit of others. Anyone of us, every one of us has our ups and downs. It is the role itself which is granted too much power that is the problem.

If we take this example from a more simple time when this beautiful planet was still pure and unpolluted, and replace "My" with "Our". And replace "King" with "Elected Representative(s)", and remember the lesson about injustice, that is not too far from what kind of place I would want to live. The whole execution thing is unjust by the way.

Think about what kind of society you would like to live in.

It is the responsibility of the community to make sure everyone's basic needs are met first. Period. We will build a life and civilization upon that foundation.

I am a big fan of Peace. But I am willing to risk my life to fight to protect that Peace if absolutely necessary. Even if there were somehow Peace on Earth someday in the future, Human experience over millions of years tells me that our society must be always vigilant. This is a big universe and time and space are not the barriers some of you might think they are. Our species has very real enemies on and off this planet. You can trust me on this.

NEVER FORGET!

While it sucks to have to deal with, it is why pure anarchy is not in our best interest, however desirable it may be.

Short of that, we have to serve each other and have mutual respect to survive.

Chapter 5
Justice?

Before going into the next chapter where the structure of government is defined, I want to address the issue of Justice, because it does not exist today.

In the former united States, the entire judicial process has been twisted and perverted to the point where only members of a private club, the B.A.R. Association (British Accredited Registry), of a foreign power control the whole process for extortion and profit. Some call this the Judicial Mafia.

In order to prevent this distortion, abuse and tyranny, anyone involved in the court process, and anyone who might be elected or appointed to a representative body or office, or otherwise serve in government, must be compelled under penalty of law, including threat of expulsion from the society, to come clean about any and all group or organizational affiliations. Right #18 needs to be applied vigorously.

While it is a right to create and join a group, that does not prevent law which would ban members of from holding office. Membership and even former membership in an organization which has oaths or commitments that have even the perception of corrupting the offices of government is cause for in-eligibility for office. I am talking about secret loyalty oaths in particular. Laws could be

passed to prevent even former members of such organizations for a specified period of time after renouncing membership, from serving in government.

By full disclosure, however, such laws do not need to be
created as the People will decide with their informed vote.
It is just a simple fact of history that secret and not so
secret societies have taken over entire nations and have
used that capacity to act against the People.

Any secret affiliations of members of government must be
treated as treason on the face of it. I am talking about
formal secret organizations or clubs. Not belief systems
or philosophy.

The former united States has devolved into a fascist police
state where millions of citizens languish in prison or on
parole for merely political and trivial reasons. A Pew
Center on States announced that in 2008 at least 2.3 Million were currently imprisoned at a cost of $49 Billion. I
am pretty sure that does not count the "secret prisons". It
does not count all the People killed by police. I does not
count the many millions more who have been imprisoned
the years before or since. I have seen numbers as low as
5% have actually committed a violent crime. Even these,
how many were self defense? It is big business. It is an
abomination. I think it is over half the population has
been arrested or harassed and or beaten by police at least
once in their lives. I was all but murdered by a sociopath
cop in San Diego when I was serving in the Navy. No,
there was not even the slightest provocation and I was
with about eight other men who witnessed this.

It would be a just act to destroy these prisons and release the victims. This issue really, pisses me off. It has to stop. You sick individuals who play prison guard need to decide if you are in support of freedom and justice and take appropriate action or just deserve to be charged and tried for your crimes against humanity. There is nothing much more contemptible than a for profit private prison or the many business who exploit the victims of this criminal enterprise for cheap labor.

All of the drug possession and use laws are an abomination. In countries all over this planet, illegitimate governments routinely execute people for drug or plant or even fungus possession, distribution and sale. I could write a whole set of books on just that subject.

The imprisonment of an individual must be an extreme last resort. It can only be justly considered in circumstances where the individual is determined by a fair hearing to be an immediate threat to the health and safety of another or the community itself. Even then, the objective needs to be the healing of the person who has gone so far astray.

Police world wide summarily execute people. That is a big reason why the right to self defense, to protect others and to keep and bear arms shall not be abolished. These individuals seem to serve the whims of the oligarchs like mindless automatons. Guess what their masters want to and are replacing them with? Yup, robots, mindless robots. Cause of thing called free will in Humans Being, they fear their minions will wake up and implement justice on them. I suggest they hurry and wake up.

This crap of being arrested and imprisoned for political and trivial acts, even "thought crimes" has only made the police force the subject of scorn, hatred and contempt by decent people. Though the Sheriff is an elected office with great power, they generally always cower to the will of some corrupt, sociopath judge. They should be arresting these traitors.

The truth is mixed, some candidates for employ by the various police forces are selected *because* they are sociopath. Others, especially older police joined to perform a vital and legitimate public service. These guys often have their hands tied and are not allowed to fulfill their just role. An officer of the People has to be able to exercise their judgment to be effective and serve the public interest.

Messed up, illegitimate laws are most of the problem. But it is important that men and women worthy of the trust the role entails are selected and promoted. All police need to be monitored by the society. Cameras, microphones, video, holographic recording, you name it. Shine the light on the public officials for their own protection. If they act justly in the Public Trust, the People will protect them. If they do not, justice will seek them out.

What I consider corrupt is not just the taking of bribes, but using the office to conspire against and violate the Rights of the People. When People peaceably assemble and a militarized force is organized, with their violent, mentally and spiritually sick agent provocateurs, this is very high crime.

I realize that most of the readers and listeners already know. About 15% of us are not as easily mind controlled. This book is speaking to the enlightened among us but it is also for the remaining 85% who are waking from their electromagnetic and chemically induced walking dream.

Everyone is an individual and liberation comes one person at a time. So a word for those of you deep in the belly of the Beast: At what point are you who are part of this criminal operation going to stand up for yourself, your family, your fellow Humans Being? When will you destroy the "command center" and refuse to blindly serve the sick reptile minded traitors? Um, they will turn on you too. You do know that? Right?

Are you a coward at heart? Cause it looks like that to the whole planet. The brave are the People you are attacking. We all know it. Do you not want to break free of the crushing mind control you have been attacked and manipulated by? Did you know that in all organized attacks on the People, the minions who were conned into these criminal acts are almost always executed by their masters? Study history of Russia, Germany, China and others. Then know you are serving the very same masters who killed hundreds of millions in those "social revolutions". What happened always happens after your role is played. You who are the enforcers, who for obvious reasons cannot be trusted, were next.

Some of you were real people at one time, free thinking, independent souls who yearned for freedom. It is within your reach, but you have to defeat the enemy within. What if you just crossed the line and joined the People? Send a message of your courage and strength that way. Of course you will have to do something meaningful, something tactical to gain the respect of the People. I am not asking you to harm anyone, just come up with a creative way to stop these attacks on We the People. We all must do our part.

While on the subject of justice, I have to say a word about non-violence. I am a man of Peace. Plain and simple. That is how I want it to be. I hope you can accept that. I am becoming a small minority. The sleeping giant has been awoken. If the actual Humans Being who blindly serve their reptilian masters cannot deal with me and those like me, you can deal with those who can no longer hold it in and are compelled to counter attack. They know who you are. As you know, there are no secrets. I will only spread information. Since they are acting in self defense, there is no real penalty for them.

Do you realize that hundreds of millions of people have no retreat? I cannot stop them any more than you can. Think before it is too late for you. It is not like you have anything going for you. You have nothing to gain where you are at. When you finally get it, this is an inter-species war, and guess what? You are way more like me than them. How do you think this will play out? Even if you win, you lose. Because the individuals who you serve know that you are a Human Being and they only appear to be. Psychics can see their real form. When the power grid goes down and the electromagnetic matrix collapses, so will everyone. If you think I don't know, then why am I risking my temporal body to tell you?

I know the value of a person who has been deep in the counsel of the enemy and chooses to be forgiven, chooses their freedom. You are valuable assets to the cause of our species.

There is a very interesting person name Ineila Benz. She has incarnated on this planet at this time to help to raise the vibrational frequency of this entire Gaia organism whose body we exist within. I recommend finding her work. I may help to mellow things out on both sides.

In the United States, and from what I can tell most of the world as well, Judges have de-facto immunity from prosecution for their treasonous acts. This is absolutely not acceptable. It can and will come to an end. Their end it looks like. Just saying what I see. I am convinced it is only through conspiracy that this has happened in the first place.

It is much more egregious for a person appointed to a position of public trust to violate the Rights of the People than someone who is not in the role of public trust. Therefore the restitution and/or other penalty should be greater for those individuals. That also means a person cannot be compelled against their will to serve in a posi tion of public trust.

No public official shall enjoy any greater Rights or privileges than is enjoyed by the People. This business of a judge dressing in robes or weird wigs and such, sitting higher and being made inaccessible to the People is inherently unjust and unacceptable. All the judge can legitimately do is conduct the hearing, manage it, and make recommendations to the jury, which always need to be there.

The facade has worn off. The illusion of legitimacy has disappeared. Judges and prosecutors are the most corrupt of all public officials today. Police are all too often their enabling tools. They also enable the criminal, treasonous acts of the legislature and executive branches. The judicial systems in most of the world are beneath contempt, I cannot call this branch of government Judicial. The hyper-inflated ego of these judges. I have to stop. My anger overflows.

No jury or judge should conform to the letter of the law if they deem it unjust. That is the whole point of a trial by jury. Law exists to serve the People, not the other way around. If it appears to be unjust, then it should not be applied or nullified altogether. Keeping public records of all hearings world wide will help clean up bad laws. Laws can be made with the best of intentions and turn out to be impractical or to be not such a good idea in actual practice.

No matter how screwed up the individual is though, there needs to be some way for them to make their restitution and / or complete their penalty. We all need a chance at redemption when we screw up. Just this policy alone would eliminate the motivation for some crimes of desperation.

Along this line of reasoning, what is up with people who want to make more and more laws with greater punishments? In this country, law is arbitrarily applied, which is to say there is no rule of law here. These people must believe that the crap they consider law only applies to others and not themselves. Unfortunately, that turns out to be all too true.

Because there is no real recourse to legitimate law, even I have to fight the real motivation to take matters into my own hands. But then, I become the bad guy, right? My patience is wearing thin, and I am a man of peace, so I am sure others feel compelled to cross that line and more will every day.

But that is all part of the plan. As David Icke eloquently points out it is like this: Create the problem, Cause a reaction, and then be ready with a Solution. This "Solution" inevitably advances the agenda of the criminal cabal who created the problem. The agenda is depopulation of 85% of We the People and to microchip and enslave the survivors. Been going on for a while now. I am sure those of you who are not too fluoridated up are already well aware of this.

This is a word of warning to those who want to use violence in reaction to the horrible injustice you have experienced. Not only have you been provoked and manipulated into that response, but what do think will be created?

The end does not justify the means. The means is an end in itself. Violence occurs only when the imagination has failed to find a more effective and creative solution. They are out there. I challenge all of you who want to fight for truth and justice for our People to demonstrate your mental, spiritual and moral superiority. Be creative. Be effective. But if you induce too much fear in the criminal elite and their minions, they will just band together more strongly. Make sure you give them an out, a way to save face. Reduce their numbers and increase ours.

The Court System in the new Society will be much different than what everyone is confronted with today.

As you review the Structure of Government, Court System section, keep in mind that in the Spirit of Thomas Jefferson, it is better for 10 guilty persons to go free than for one innocent person to be falsely convicted.

The object of the game for me is to reduce stress. Peace reduces stress. There cannot be Peace without Justice. Less stress will reduce the motivation for aggressive and/or criminal behavior.

We can devolve into chaos, mass death and destruction or choose to create and build a new Society which works at a local and global level. One that is decentralized with checks on all forms of power to guarantee the protection and safety of the People.

Chapter 6
Governmental Structure

The goal is to create a system which is sustainable, truly Of, By and For the People. It must prevent concentration of power in the hands of a few. One which can be implemented in communities on a global scale.

This is a high level overview. The many details remain to be worked out.

Transparency

The base of power is the informed individual. To this end, government operations need to be transparent to the people they serve. There are basically three ways to accomplish this.

1)   An actual free press. We all know how a publication can spin, twist, distort, honest error and outright lie. By ensuring there is competition in the media consumers of the media will be able to discern the truth. Keep in mind there will be actual professional reporters and journalists, something Americans and other people dealing with authoritarian regimes are not used to. There will be no more quotes from unnamed "official sources". This is a pathetic fraud. Real reporters will not reprint propaganda without question, comment or analysis, as most of the world is used to now.'

To this end, consolidation of media will not be allowed. Due to the different economic model, a single individual will not own or control any organization. All members of an organization, will have say in the running of their place of work.

An organization would not be allowed to have more than one of each type of media per community or population center. That is one television, radio, newspaper, magazine, publishing house, movie production studio and theater per population center. There will likely be new forms of media developed and suppressed media technology made available, the same principals will apply.

2) All civilian government meetings, court hearings, councils, etc will be open to public view by Citizens of this Society. We currently live in a total global surveillance society. In this model, it is government that is subject to surveillance and it will not have to be hidden.

The military has legitimate need for operational secrecy, but it is subject to civilian government resource allocation control and oversight. It will not be an offense for a member of our military organization to report criminal wrong doing to members of our legislature or executive branch.

Branches of Government

The Constitution of the united States defines three branches of government. Many other nations have an executive, legislative and court system branch. Even when three branches are not clearly defined, these roles still exist.

Of, By and For the People

Our Society will have four separate branches of government, with two tiers, local and global. The global body will not have direct taxation authority except inter-planetary commerce. Otherwise the Global Government will be funded by money creation and revenues paid by Local Area Governments. The primary need for taxation will be to fund the single planetary military and global infrastructure.

These four branches are: Executive, Legislative, Courts and Fair Witness.

No individual may serve in more than one branch of government or the military at the same time. This must be strictly enforced, a choice must be made publicly when this situation occurs.

The first tier or Local Area Government is made up of all four branches. The second tier, the Global Government is both representative of the Local Area Governments and the People for the entire planet. This will also have four branches, however the roles and responsibilities are different.

This flattened hierarchy model will maximize efficiency and control by Citizens. It is important to minimize regional factionalism. To this end, the main purpose of the Global Government will be to resolve disputes and prevent conflict between Local Area Governments. A middle tier of government would serve no useful purpose and further distance the People from a more representative government at the global level. Middle tiers would also compete for authority allotted to the Local Area and

Global governmental bodies and add dramatically to the cost of government.

Cost efficiency of government is critical. What we are used to today will become a dark period in our history, not to be repeated. The pay for government officials must be consistent with the rest of society. If the pay is too high, the position may be coveted, if the pay is too low, the most qualified may remain in the private sector.

The intent is Local Area Government for each major population center which would include rural populations in the surrounding area. Boundaries are to be based on one primary factor, the ratio of representation between the citizen and their governing areas. In areas of high population density, for instance along coastlines, there will be more Local Area Governments than in less densely populated areas. The size in population should not exceed 20,000,000, or be smaller than 2,000,000. These number cannot be fixed at this time, but experience, practicality and public discourse will produce proper ratios.

The most densely populated areas, the biggest cities of today, are a tremendous burden on resources. There can be no mandate to force People to relocate. When the current gross injustice in wealth inequality is no longer a problem, as our social structures are implemented, People will have more options to relocate as desired. I predict less population density will be one of the results.

One factor that exists and is likely to increase dramatically is the mobility of the population. When there is an election, a citizen must be able to vote in whatever local area they currently reside. Migratory groups will not lack representation. Elections for the Global Government will not be a problem as Citizenship is for the single planetary government.

With implementation of suppressed energy technology, it will be easier for planned communities to develop in currently uninhabited areas, further reducing population density by offering quality alternatives. High speed global public transit will also contribute to more diffuse population centers.

Current political borders should be disregarded. Most are completely arbitrary and not natural. Using natural boundaries such as coastlines, rivers and mountain ranges is practical. Using ethnic populations in defining local areas of government is not a valid criteria and does not promote peace.

If a Local Area Government gets too big, it would be possible for it to divide itself into two Local Area Governments. It would take a full public vote put to the People by the Legislature and approval of the Executive. Such a move would require a two thirds majority.

The following is a very minimal outline. It is a bit outside the scope of this book to go beyond that. I will be happy to flesh in more detail in subsequent articles and books. This outline is to provide a minimal working model and promote widespread discussion. I will likely be dead soon, whether is it today or 20 years from now, this gift is for those who will live in it. Input, consensus building, etc. has to happen.

Of, By and For the People

Concerning null and void Treaties. It has come to my attention that various non-human groups have made "secret treaties" with various illegitimate governments. They are generally in the form of technology in exchange for the abductions of We the People. Some victims have suffered horribly and then been eaten. Some have been used in all manner of genetic experiments. Some have it even worse, their souls are literally captured electromagnetically and imprisoned. In all of these, We the People are considered exploitable property.

Not only are these treaties made with the worst criminal elements, not all of which are Humans Being themselves by the way, but any Treaty or agreement made in secret is automatically a fraud and non-binding on We the People. Any Treaty or agreement made that violates our Declared Rights is null and void on the face of it. These malevolent entities use the agreements to con and deceive the fools they made them with. They act as though somehow these criminal acts have been made acceptable with willing consent. But they are not acceptable and the People have not consented. We are NOT Property. We the People are at war with these piece of shit entities operating through subterfuge and deceit.

Chapter 7

Executive Branch

The Executive branch of government is primarily admin-istrative in nature.

All meetings need to have the presence of the Certified Fair Witness or Witnesses as appropriate.

It is responsible for:

1)   Protecting the Natural Environment. While any Citizen has the right to seek a hearing for environmental pollution, this would happen only when the Executive administration has failed in its responsibility. If the administration consistently fails in its duty, the appropri-ate individuals may be recalled from office or appoint-ment. The positions would be filled again, with greater scrutiny.

Such abominations of nature as fracking which is basi-cally designed for the purpose of destroying underground aquifers and creating geologic instability; clear cutting of forests which destroys too much habitat and disregards the role of trees, especially old trees, which create weather stability among other things; mining operations which are too destructive such as mountain top removal or large scale strip mining; application of toxic chemicals to farms; runoff of waste to the point of polluting lakes and streams; toxic waste from manufacturing; electromagnetic pollution and more; all fall under the role of Protecting the Natural Environment.

This is not intended to stop extraction of natural resources, but to make such extraction conform to standards which are respectful of life. Better living through technology.

It may be impossible to prevent the creation, in practical terms, of toxic substances. But these toxic substances must be rendered stable or broken down to safe components using technology before release into our natural environment. Clean up of the existing horrors which have been inflicted also need to be performed or coordinated by the Executive.

2)   Tracking of all Citizens for the purpose making sure they receive their payment from the Treasury. Ensuring payments are not intercepted, extorted or made in error. Citizens do not have to have legal names. Each individual has a unique vibrational frequency. Papers and other forms of identification such as micro-chipping are not required or allowed to even be considered. We are all currently monitored by satellite by our unique wave signature. This technology will be captured and applied to beneficial use.

3)   Ensuring free and fair elections take place on schedule and by process as defined by the Legislature. Voting rights cannot be taken away as punishment. This has been used as a political tool routinely in the former united States and other countries. If there are so many prisoners that anyone is worried they have a vote, that is

all the more reason why they need a vote.

Fund raising for political campaigns by elected officials will not be allowed. History has proven over and over again that there is really no more of a corrupting influence on government than this. Political Campaigns will be conducted in the Public Space and by the willing acts of Citizens who may speak, wear signage on clothing, write, publish, etc. There are many ways to conduct a political campaign without the massive fraud, waste, abuse and political corruption some of us know all too well today.

I am sick of the pathetic truth the we get the best government money can buy. This has to stop. And it has to stop on a global scaled to be effective.

The Executive, in ensuring free and fair elections will provide and ensure open public forums for debate. No candidate will be excluded for lack of currency. The disenfranchised and outcasts will no longer be. Political party affiliation cannot be required to run for elected office. A level field of play will allow Citizens from all walks of life and all ethnicity an even chance to campaign, to be heard, to get elected to office.

4)   Collecting moneys as appropriate by legislation for the public Treasury.

5)   Full public accounting of all Treasury accounts and spending.

6)   Ensuring the Rights of the People are protected.

7)   The Executive has the duty to veto any legislation which it deems to violate the Rights of the People. This is the second check on bad law.

8)   Implementing processes, organizations, and infrastructure projects as per appropriate legislation. Some public service jobs will be employees of the Executive. Some will be performed by chartered organizations where the Executive, with prior Legislative authority will setup, staff and launch these chartered organization which will then be more or less autonomous.

9)   Performing a police role including criminal investigation using technology when necessary. Police will not have authority to issue orders to Citizens. They will be generally respectful to and in return respected and supported by the People.

10)   Enforcing the will of the Courts.

11)   Take responsibility for prisoners and the healing needed to complete their restitution and penalty. When a Citizen has completed their penalty, the role of the executive will be judged by how well the convicted person is able to restore themselves into public Society. A civilization may be effectively judged by the conditions of their prisons and by how few prisoners there are. There will be no such thing as a for profit or private prison. Prisoners will not be treated like slaves or cheap labor for profit.

12)   Be responsible for Prisoners of war. Maltreatment is not allowed and will be a punishable offense. This reflects on our whole Society. It has dramatic effect regarding the length and even intensity of a conflict.

Local Area Government Executive Branch

Here are the primary offices of the Executive. These offices are directly elected by the People of the Local Area Government on the regular three year election cycle.

First Executive:

Senior administrator of the Executive Branch of the Local Area Government, its services, facilities and operations.

Does not have authority to remove elected officials from office.

Recommends two candidates for the Global Legislative Senate to Local Area Legislature for approval to represent the Local Area Government.

May Sign or Veto bills or laws approved by the Local Area Government House of Representative.

Second Executive:

Fills in for First Executive when needed. Is elected on the same ticket as First Executive. Usually the one who does the real work. While their boss is giving speeches or making public ceremonial appearances.

Treasurer:

Maintains the Public Treasury.

Ensures proper accounting, spending, payments and keeps public records on all monies.

Administers taxation as appropriate by law.

Sheriff:

Basically the top law enforcement administrator in whose department police authority is vested. This includes criminal investigation.

Environmental Protector:

Responsible for the proper access to natural resources.

Proactively tests and monitors for pollution.

Receives environmental complaints from Citizens which may result in further investigation.

Initiates and Conducts environmental complaint investigations.

Ensures weather modification technology is applied in the best interest of all Citizens within the Local Area Government. This includes making sure destructive storms miss population centers and are reduced in intensity if needed for the safety of Citizens. Pretty much the opposite of how the technology is used today.

<u>Global Government Executive Branch</u>

Responsible for global infrastructure and projects.

Space exploration and other civilian off-planet operations.

Facilitate trade with other civilizations on, in or off planet.

Protect the Rights of the People.

The Global Government Executive branch will consist of the following elected offices:

First Executive:

Senior administrator of the Executive Branch of the Global Government, its services, facilities and operations.

Does not have authority to remove elected officials from office.

Appoints Senior Military Officer pending approval of the Global Legislative Senate.

Primary civilian oversight of the Military.

May Sign or Veto bills or laws approved by the Global Legislature.

Second Executive:

Fills in for First Executive when needed. Is elected on the same ticket as First Executive. Usually the one who does the real work. While their boss is giving speeches or making public ceremonial appearances.

Treasurer:

Maintains the Public Treasury.

Ensures proper accounting, spending, payments and keeps public records on all monies.

Administers taxation as appropriate by law.

Administers payment to all Citizens.

Secretary of Embassy

Senior Diplomat.

Political role which represents the Planetary Government of Humans Being to other civilizations and planetary governments, councils and such.

Appoints Ambassadors to other Civilizations on, in and off planet.

Hosts foreign dignitaries and official envoys.

Reports to the First Executive, the Senate and House of Representatives of the Global Government.

Coordinates management of all Embassies and staff.

Facilitates embassy communications and communications security.

Coordinates with the military to protect and secure embassies.

Submit Treaties for approval to the Global Legislature. Sign or veto approved Treaties before being put to a two thirds vote for approval by all of the Citizens.

Sheriff:

Responsible for the police role within the Global Government. If a district is created to host said government, would have police authority within that district.

Responsible for coordination with the local Sheriffs for Inter-Local Area Government crime and/or criminal investigation.

Ensures best practices are shared between Local Area Government Sheriff departments.

Liaison with other civilization's police authority.

Criminal investigation authority within the Global Government.

Environmental Protector:

Responsible for coordinating the proper access to natural resources were those resources are between or across Local Area Governments.

First point of dispute resolution regarding resources between Local Area Governments.

Coordinates global resources such as ocean fishing management for example, based on objective criteria.

Responsible for Environmental Protection in areas of this planet outside of any Local Government Area.

Proactively tests and monitors for pollution on a global scale. Includes the consolidation of data collected by the Local Environmental Protectors. Ensures the free flow of such information and access to all Citizens.

Receives environmental complaints from Citizens which may result in further investigation on a global scale.

Initiates and Conducts environmental investigations on a global scale.

Ensures weather modification technology is applied in the best interest of all Citizens across the Local Area Governments. This includes making sure major or destructive storms miss population centers and are reduced in intensity if needed for the safety of Citizens. Pretty much the opposite of how the technology is used today.

The main difference between the Global and Local Area Environmental Protector is it deals on a planetary scale versus a local scale.

Chapter 8
Legislative Branch

The Legislative Branch of government will have two tiers. A House of Representatives for each Local Area Government and the Global Government. The Global Government will also have a Senate to represent the Local Area Governments.

All laws passed must conform to the Rights of the People without exception.

This is not a parliament. All officials elected to office hold their seats. Not a number of seats per political party whose occupancy is assigned by that political party. Candidates do not have to have any party affiliation.

Each Legislative body has authority to appoint its officers, create sub-committees and set its rules of operation.

The large number of seats in the Houses of Representatives is essential to proper representation of the People. The inherent inefficiencies are on purpose to restrict the creation of new laws.

The Legislature has authority to set rules for and authorization of Chartered Organizations within their jurisdictions.

The Legislature is the main governing and decision making body.

All hearings must be public or the proceeding published or made public soon after.

All meetings are null and void without the presence of the Certified Fair Witness or Witnesses as appropriate.

The Houses of Representatives have authority to define representative districts for seats in the house. These districts must be simple defined areas, no contorted districts.

Each Legislative body has authority to conduct investigative hearings relative to their jurisdictions, and compel witnesses to appear.

Each Legislative body is responsible for resource allocation within their jurisdiction.

The Local Area Government House of Representatives:

Represents the People of that Local Area Government.

Members will be directly elected with one representative per 20,000 adult Citizens. The number of seats may change with each election cycle based on demographics. The Legislature does not have the authority to arbitrarily reduce or increase the number of seats.

The elections will take place every three years on the normal election cycle. The entire House will be up for election at each cycle.

This legislative body is charged with passing spending legislation which it is the duty of the executive to implement after signing if not vetoed.

Spending cycles may be annual, bi-annual or tri-annual as determined by each Local Area Legislature.

Major office appointments by the First Executive are subject to approval of the Legislative House (Local Area Government).

Has power to impeach members of the Local Area Government Executive and Court System for cause.

Global Government Legislature

Military oversight and resource allocation.

All manner of Global Standards including weights, measures and time keeping. This includes setting up a new calendar. May create and charter measurement standards organization(s) subject to control of the People.

Laws which define the details of the Governmental Structure and Procedure.

Laws of Global Commerce.

Laws of Global Infrastructure.

Charter organizations whose primary operations are in space, inner Earth, Outer Space or which provide services on a planetary scale or otherwise beyond the scope of Local Area Government.

Authorize currency creation on an annual, bi-annual or tri-annual basis.

Will consist of two bodies:

Global Senate:

Represents the Local Area Governments.

Candidates will have been nominated by the First Executive and voted for approval by the Local Area Government Legislature and serve a six year term.

Each Local Area Government will have two Senate seats, regardless of their populations. These may vote for each other in the case of absence of one, with their consent.

One of the two seats will be up for appointment every three years alternately. Appointment to this body will occur 30 days prior to the standard election cycle. The reasoning is officials will have had three years to know more what is going on. Provides stability and continuity.

Approve major administrative appointments of the First Executive and Ambassador appointments of the Secretary of Embassy.

Hold impeachment hearings of the elected offices of the Global Executive and Judicial branch.

Must approve or not any legislation passed to it after approval by the Global House of Representatives.

Approval of Treaties drafted and approved by the First Executive by a two thirds majority before sending to the Global House of Representatives.

Global House of Representatives:

This house will represent the People with one seat for every 2,000,000 (two million) adult Citizens. If the population is 5 billion, that is 2,500 representatives.

The number of seats may change with each election cycle if the voting population changes. Due to the way public records will be kept, and the Fair Witness branch of government, these numbers will always be publicly available and known.

All spending laws must originate with this body, then sent to the Senate for approval.

Approval of Treaties passed by the Global Senate by a two thirds majority which are then submitted to the Secretary of Embassy.

Chapter 9
Court System Branch

The Court System must be transparent and open to the public. There will be no such thing as secret evidence or testimony.

This Court System will have Conductors of the Court and Public Arbitrators. They will be in charge of the Court process and conducting hearings.

There are three types of Court in this system. A Certified Fair Witness will be assigned to each Court and must be present for any proceeding to take place.

Major Court:

Where a Citizen is charged with a serious offense, as defined by the Legislature. This could result in serious penalty and restitution.

Minor Court:

Where a Citizen is charged with a minor offense, as defined by the Legislature. This could result in minor penalty and restitution.

Contract Court:

This is where issues between Parties who have a contractual dispute or other disagreement which needs to be resolved are heard.

This court has no Jury, Rights of the People Guarantor or defendant. An elected skilled Arbitrator will be presented with the case and render a decision. That decision will be binding.

With our two tiered system of government, each Local Area Government will have jurisdiction within their area. The structures defined below pertain to the Local Area Government.

Conductor of the Court:

This is an elected office. Elections for Conductor of the Court will be held on the standard three year cycle, with approximately half of the offices up on each cycle.

Each term will be for a period of six years. This is to provide stability, promote impartiality and professionalism. They must be selected for integrity and leadership skills. There will be no term limits. If a community finds a good Conductor of the Court, they will want to keep them in that office for as long as they are willing to serve.

The Conductor of the Court will be expected to keep up on legislation.

They will not write Rulings. Each case will come down to a vote of the Jury. They will not interpret law as now, because the laws will be short, simple and in clear language as per the Rights of the People.

The Conductor of the Court will wear a Colored Sash to denote their role and the type of court they are conducting as determined by the Legislature.

Each Conductor of the Court will have authority to make recommendations to the Legislature as to whether a law should be modified or abolished based on their practical experience and expertise.

Each Conductor of the Court will have full authority to manage the process including:

Determining in which type of court the case should be heard.

Advise the jury, clarify issues and answer their questions.

Dismiss a case, even abolish a Jury Ruling if they determine that to be the just course of action. This may also be required in the case gross Jury misconduct. That is why it is an elected office. Someone has to be in a position to make that call to prevent injustice. They cannot have their hands tied and be expected to deliver on the promise of Justice.

The authority to have a Jury member or spectator removed from the hearing for misconduct.

The authority to declare a mistrial for cause and a new hearing convened as soon as possible. If there is a schedule of court hearing, this retrial must take priority.

Rights of the People Guarantor:

This is an Elected office with elections held on the standard three year election cycle.

Has investigative authority and presents evidence to a Warrant Jury within the Local Area Government when a violation of Rights, which is a crime, occurs.

Is the watchdog of the Sheriff and other Executive Branch officials for the People to protect from abuse of office.

May presents evidence for impeachment of a Local Area Government official to be removed from office to the legislative body.

Public Arbitrator:

This is an elected office with elections held on the standard three year election cycle. No term limits should be imposed. If a community finds a talented Public Arbitrator, they will want to keep them in that office for as long as they are willing to serve.

Presides over Contract Court.

The Public Arbitrator will wear a Colored Sash to denote their role as determined by the Legislature.

Each Public Arbitrator will have authority to manage the process including:

Dismiss a case if they determine that to be the just course of action.

The authority to have a Person removed from the hearing for misconduct.

Major and Minor Court structure:

Each Major and Minor Court will have an attendant from the Executive Branch, in a police role to support the Conductor of the Courts and enforce the decision of the Jury.

In a Major Court the Jury will consist of nine Citizens plus three alternates. The alternates would only vote in a replacement role. This is to cover dismissals and excused absences like hospital, family emergency and such.

In a Minor Court the Jury will consist of five Citizens plus two alternates.

Both Courts will also have:

A Guarantor of Rights and their staff.

One Certified Fair Witness, who may have an apprentice and/or staff assistant.

One defendant at a time please for the sake of fairness.

Warrant Jury

A Warrant Jury will be empaneled from the normal Jury pool, on an as needed basis for the purpose of issuing Warrants. It will consist of nine Citizens.

This process should not take long so no alternate jurors are necessary.

A Rights of the People Guarantor convenes the Warrant Jury.

A Certified Fair Witness must be in attendance.

Evidence and testimony will be presented to them by a Rights of the People Guarantor on behalf of an injured party. The jurors may question the witnesses. If it appears insufficient information is presented, the jury should vote against issuing a warrant.

For a Warrant to be issued, it must be clearly based upon probable cause that Rights have been violated. It must be supported by oath or affirmation. It must particularly describe the place to be searched, and the persons or things to be seized.

If a Warrant is issued, it is handed over to the Executive Branch representative who is acting in a police role.

It will take a vote with two thirds majority to issue a Warrant for search and/or seizure or a Warrant for Arrest and/or for charges to be brought against a Citizen compelling them to appear in a Major or Minor Court.

While these hearing may be conducted without a public audience, all evidence and accusation must be made public soon after the fact.

The accused has the Right to be informed of the nature and cause of the accusation. The accused has the Right to be confronted with the witnesses against him in a Major or Minor Court.

Reasonable Search and/or Seizure and Arrest

A Warrant is required for search and/or seizure of evidence. A separate Warrant is required for the arrest of a Citizen.

Keep in mind that each Citizen may be located anywhere on the globe by their unique wave signature using satellite technology. There is little fear of escape from justice.

In our Society, casual arrest is not allowed. Because of the comprehensive nature of tracking technology these proper safeguards must be in place and respected.

At some point in the near future, I sincerely believe based on my own analysis, that psychic powers of mind will exceed even the best physical tracking technology. It will become very difficult for anyone to commit a crime against another without being made known.

Major and Minor Court procedure:

The accused has the Right to be confronted with the witnesses against him in a Major or Minor Court.

All hearings need to be held as soon as is reasonable. The hearing need to be short, not long and drawn out.

The accused shall have the right to a fair hearing. This means, by an impartial Jury with due process as is outlined. The accused, will have a compulsory process for obtaining witnesses who might prove or aid their defense.

The accused has the Right to the Assistance of Counsel for their defense. Their choice of Counsel shall not be limited to members of any-group or organization, but be a person who is a member of this Society, is willing and is chosen by the accused for their defense.

Any evidence and witnesses must be made known to each side at least three working days before a hearing. Longer if deemed necessary by the Conductor of the Court.

The accused person may not be compelled to testify and may refuse to answer specific questions which may implicate themselves even when they do testify.

Anyone who is found to knowingly present false evidence or testimony or withhold key evidence should be charged with a criminal offense. The severity of the offense is relative to the severity of the of the case being heard. Proper procedures need to be followed and a Warrant Jury presented with evidence first.

There will be opening and closing statements by both sides.

Each side may call witnesses which may be questioned by both sides alternately.

The Conductor of the Court may question witnesses as in their role, they may have the wisdom to ask discerning questions missed by others. This is not a game between members of a private club where the actual Citizens are more like spectators and have little or no say. The object of the Court is justice, not financial gain like it is today.

Active members of the Jury may submit written questions for witnesses to the Conductor of the Court.

The Jury will remove to a private room or area to deliberate. A Certified Fair Witness will be in attendance.

The Conductor of the Court may be called in to answer questions, but would not attend the jury deliberations.

The Conductor of the Court may review the record of the Certified Fair Witness and even ask objective questions regarding the conduct of the Jury. This is a final check on Jury misconduct.

The Jury would vote as to whether the Defendant is found in violation of the charges against them.

In Major Court, a majority of eight is required to find the accusations made of the defendant are true.

In Minor Court, it will take four of the five votes to find the accusations made of the defendant are true.

If the accusations are found to be true, the accused has the duty to make restitution to the injured party and may face a penalty as previously and narrowly determined by the Legislature.

Excessive, cruel and unusual punishments may not be inflicted, including maiming and physical abuse.

In all matters of dispute resolution, the objective has to be for healing. All involved parties should be better off as a result.

In no case will fines be levied or property seized that does not go toward restitution. That is a court cannot charge for its services or have a financial incentive to convict.

Clearing a False Conviction

Cases may be brought to the appropriate Court for the purpose of clearing a conviction. In this matter, a Warrant Jury is presented evidence or testimony. This should include evidence or testimony not known or available in the original hearing. If the Jury determines a reasonable case can be made that a conviction has been made in error, Declaration for Hearing will be made to that effect.

Any Citizen may request a Rights of Citizens Guarantor to convene a Warrant Jury for this purpose. If they refuse, the next step is to present the information to a

Local Area Government Representative who may convene a Warrant Jury.

If it is determined the refusal was an obstruction of justice, the Rights of Citizens Guarantor is subject to impeachment and a Warrant may issued for their arrest.

If it is determined there was foul play which resulted in a false conviction, proper Warrants for search and seizure and arrest will be issued. This applies to all public officials and Citizens alike.

The defending Person may be cleared of a conviction when it is determined to have been made in error by a Major or Minor Court, depending on which court the conviction was made.

Minor and Major Court Jury of Citizens

Citizens will serve on a Jury for a period of 90 to 120 days. The extended time is to account for ongoing hearing where a Juror has passed 90 days. They may be chosen by lottery from the pool of eligible Citizens as defined by the Legislature. All adult Citizens who are not serving in government or military are potentially eligible.

When one has served on a Jury, they should not have to do it again until ever other eligible person has served. For individuals who like to serve on a Jury, the Legislature should determine an appropriate interval before they are eligible to be in the Jury lottery.

If selected, they would take a leave of absence from their other activities. The Legislature will specifically define exceptions. These exception may include competency; age such as being too young or too senior to have to serve; Persons who have or are currently dealing with prior charges against them; Conflict of Interest; Persons in Hospital; and such.

Selected Jurors will be able to request to get out of duty, but must have a very good reason. The decision will be made by the Conductor of the Court. They will be returned to the Jury lottery pool.

The Shape of the Major and Minor Courts.

I recommend a semi-circle, where, from inside the arc, the Conductor of the Court sits to the Jury's left, at a modest desk. The Jury will sit in seats in a row making up the arc.

Facing this arc, there will be two rectangular tables at a 45 degree angle to the center with a wide gap between them.

A seat in the middle facing the Jury and Conductor of the Court. This is where the witnesses and defendant will sit when they are providing testimony and/or being questioned.

On the left will be the Guarantor of Rights who will present the case and attempt to prove the charges brought against the defendant. Injured parties will be at the table or near it as is practical.

On the right will be the Person who is charged and is defending and their Counsel who may also have staff assistants.

Contract Court

In this Court, both parties voluntarily solicit the Court for dispute resolution. The elected Public Arbitrator will preside. This is like a private arbitration today except it will not cost the parties involved to have a hearing. There is no, jury, Guarantor of Rights or executive branch representative, but there is a Certified Fair Witness.

This certainly does not preclude private arbitration. It is designed to provide valid dispute resolution for such minor things as petty theft, neighbor disputes, car accidents and such. Non-criminal disputes. Disputes that are not worth the time or cost of Minor Court.

Because Contract Court is a necessary government service provided by the Court System, the presence of the Certified Fair Witness will make the proceeds and resultant ruling by the Public Arbitrator public.

So, if a vendor or merchant or individual takes a party to this court for petty theft, it still goes on their public record. The Legislature would have to set the threshold for petty theft versus serious theft.

Please keep in mind that with all the other stuff in place, there will not be much crime in this Society. In the case of petty theft or minor injury, if the defendant party refuses to appear in Contract Court, the next step is the Minor Court process. This could be used as leverage to get a settlement.

Global Government Court

At the Global Government level, the Court is very different. First, there is only a Major Court.

The Conductor of the Court is elected by sitting Conductors of the Court from the Local Government level. The nominee must have served at least one full term as a Conductor of the Court at the local level. The nominees does not have to be active, just have completed at least one full six year term.

Three Certified Fair Witnesses must be in attendance.

Second, the parties will be representatives of the Executive Branch of a Local Area Government. It is not a criminal court. It is intended for serious dispute resolution between Local Area Governments.

Also, it is in this court that disputes between the Global Society and Outside parties may receive a public hearing. These may be non Humans Being, other civilizations or governments.

The Jury Panel will be selected from Citizens who have served at least one term in the Global Government Legislature.

The Jury Panel will consist of twenty one Jurors and seven Alternates.

It will take a majority vote of nineteen of the twenty one Jurors to resolve the case.

The Conductor of the Court will be a person elected due to having great diplomatic skills.

The result is binding on the Local or Global Government(s). It may be a useful step in a larger dispute resolution.

There has to be actual Law, Rights or Treaty Violation in play to bring the parties to court. Else, the Global Legislature would be the proper venue for a hearing.

This is not a back-door way to make a binding Treaty to which the Society would be bound to. If, as a result of the hearing a Treaty or Treaty modification is determined to be the best solution, that Treaty would still be subject to approval by vote of all the Citizens on the Planet.

For a Treaty to be brought to a Global vote, the Global Executive and Legislature will have already signed their approval and made their recommendation.

Chapter 10
Fair Witness Branch

Thank you Robert A Heinlein. The concept of Fair Witness is presented in his book "Stranger in a Strange Land". This is a work of fiction set in the future. I am not endorsing anything in that amusing read, except the concept of Fair Witness is just too good an idea. It is a fascinating concept.

This concept is very deep actually. It resolves a key problem. Right now, the alleged government has pretty much no credibility. Governments routinely alter and erase records. Critical information is kept "secret" from the People all the time now. Usually to cover up crimes against the People. This is a global phenomena. I do not want to hear denials of that statement from existing 'government officials' except as a joke.

History has proven, over and over again, governments cannot be trusted to keep proper records on themselves. And when they do, those records are not properly accessible to the People. This fourth part of the governmental structure is a check on these abuses.

The independence of the Fair Witness branch of government will provide badly needed credibility, fairness and openness.

Individuals would be trained, tested and certified to be impartial, non-bias witnesses. Their training and testing will be difficult to complete. They will be taught to be honest and keen observers. Their language will be clear and objective without assumption or subjectivity. They will be trusted to be truthful.

The Fair Witness will be required to be fluent in all of the languages used in government. They will become linguistic masters.

The key is these individuals must remain independent of any outside control or leverage which could be used against them. Sexual blackmail cannot be allowed to remove them from office.

It will be a criminal act to influence them in any way which could compromise them. This would be a violation of the Rights where the victim is the whole Society. This is the only designated group which would have such a protective status.

They would not be required to perform any other kind of work as long as they keep their status.

Once compromised, they would lose their status.

Fair Witnesses will be the record keepers within the operations of the other three branches of government.

They will be tasked to prepare and keep meeting minutes, and all manner of records and logs as necessary.

Their role is as observers within the other three branches of government and this requires unrestricted access.

It is their duty to create and maintain a library of records for all Citizens of the Society. These libraries of records must be made freely and easily accessible to all members of Society.

Fair Witnesses are not elected and represent no-one, only the truth.

They do not have any other authority. This is not a police role.

Fair Witnesses, including panel members will be subject to recall in this manner:

Complaint of breach of trust or compromise may be initiated by any Citizen of the Society. The first step it to submit a complaint to the appropriate Fair Witness Panel. If the matter is not resolved then proceeding for removal of certification are as follows:

The First Executive at a local or global level of the executive branch may endorse a complaint against an individual Fair Witness which is determined to be valid.

A local or global House of Representatives member may also endorse a complaint against an individual Fair Witness which they determine to be valid.

This complaint would be put to a vote by the appropriate House of Representatives. The House may have a committee which would have to vote to recommend a vote by the whole House. With a majority vote to endorse, the complaint is sent to the First Executive for signature.

Only when when a Citizen complaint of breach of trust of a Fair Witness is approved by a majority vote of the House and signed by the First Executive, could a Fair Witness be stripped of their status.

To clarify, the Citizen Complaint, and the Executive and Legislative endorsement of that Complaint must occur within the same local tier governing area where the alleged violation occurred.

In the case of Citizen Complaint where the alleged violation occurred while in service within the Global tier of government, the Endorsement of the Global First Executive and Global House of Representative is required.

This is essential because it is just too easy otherwise for a Fair Witness to lose their status for political reasons.

Otherwise, a Certified Fair Witness retains that office for their natural life unless they resign or retire.

In keeping with the requirement for openness, training materials, criteria and even the training itself must be open to public inspection.

As to whether they would have the same access to the military is an open question. It does not seem desirable or practical. But it is impossible to foresee everything. Maybe there is a role there, maybe not. I propose waiting for several years before exploring the possibility of a Certified Fair Witness having a role in the Military.

Are they always on duty, like a priest or is there a way to designate on and off duty, for instance so they can socialize, vacation and such?

Obviously this group would have to be sober in to perform their duty. Being intoxicated on alcohol, opiates, or similar natural and synthetic substances would be a problem.

If they are always 'on duty' then over time, they may become too apart from the rest of society. As their role is strict, how about on duty all the time except during vacation time? Would their off time be 30 days a year or more to be fair to them?

Over time, it may evolve that this branch of government is used in non-government organizations. At this time, I would caution against that, but that discussion is outside of the present scope.

I propose the following tiered rank structure within the Fair Witness branch of government:

1)   Trainee

Qualified persons who are accepted into the program who are going through their training phase. This phase will be complete when they have passed all required course work and testing. I would expect it would take at least three years, maybe up to seven years to complete as this is a highly demanding role.

Graduates of the Fair Witness educational program will be announced in a public ceremony.

2)   Apprentice

Apprentices have completed their schooling, have passed their testing and are assigned to a Certified Fair Witness for a period of time to gain real world experience. At this time they are not ready for independent assignment.

The duration of this phase and criteria to be met will set by the Senior Fair Witness Panel.

The Mentor they are assigned to will report to the appropriate panel when the Apprentice is ready for Certification.

Fair Witnesses who complete their apprenticeship and receive Certification will be announced in a public ceremony.

3) Certified Fair Witness (CFW)

A CFW will have full rights and privileges to assume their role with the trust and confidence of the People. The may be assigned to independent duty. They will have all the appropriate access to the Executive, Courts and Legislative branches of government.

There must be some form of badge or symbol or article of attire so that their presence is openly known. The Global Fair Witness Panel has authority to determine this as well as dress or uniform standards.

Maybe a robe, a jumpsuit or a sash? It would not be appropriate to the role for these symbols or attire to be too loud or flashy. They will have such trust and their service to Society so highly respected, they can afford to be modest in their display.

4) Senior Certified Fair Witness (SCFW)

This group would be eligible to serve on Fair Witness panels.

They do not lose their status as Certified Fair Witness. However, they would be relieved of CFW duty except as needs require to temporarily fill a position pending assignment by a CFW.

A CFW would be eligible to apply for this level after a specified number of years of service. Once accepted they would receive further education as appropriate for this management role.

As this branch of government are the Librarians who keep and disseminate records. It is not in their role to restrict access to information. Someone has to manage the libraries, and People who perform day to day tasks. The day to day tasks can be performed by Citizens.

It may be necessary and practical for a CFW to have the assistance of support staff. This staff role would, of course be merit based, but be performed by Citizens. It is logical that some of the Citizens who work within the Fair Witness branch would want to apply to be a Trainee. But it could not be a requirement to serve on staff before applying for Trainee.

All staff would be hired and managed by SCFW. The CFW role is too demanding for any other duties or managerial responsibilities.

Fair Witness Panels

I propose a two tiered panel system in keeping consistent with the two tiered governmental system. These panels would oversee the administration of the branch for each Local Area Government and Global Government. They would have full authority to de-certify, repremand or order additional training of the CFWs serving within their jurisdiction.

Of, By and For the People

Global Fair Witness Panel:

There would be one panel of nine Senior Certified Fair Witnesses

This panel would consist of nine members to be responsible for the overall administration of this branch of government for the whole planet. This panel would set of criteria, training, testing, performance reviews, etc.

Members would serve staggered nine year terms.

Elections for three panel members at a time would be held at three year intervals.

Only Senior Certified Fair Witnesses are eligible to vote for Global Fair Witness Panel member.

The object of this rule is to prevent the politicization of this branch of government. The SCFW would be the most informed voters. This is also consistent with Society values in that they are electing their own leaders.

The Global Fair Witness panel would vote to select a leader each three year cycle, after the new members have been empaneled. The same person could potential hold this leadership position for a maximum of nine years.

Panel members may serve for a maximum of 12 years. This could happen for instance in the case of unexpected vacancies. When stepping down from this august body, they will still be Senior Certified Fair Witnesses.

Eligible candidates will have completed at least one term on a Local Fair Witness Panel to qualify for nomination.

Local Fair Witness Panel:

Each local government will have one Local Fair Witness Panel similar in structure to the Global Fair Witness Panel.

These panels would also consist of nine members. They are responsible for the overall administration of this branch of government for each local government. This panel would implement criteria, training, testing, performance reviews, etc. as determined by the Global Fair Witness Panel.

Members would serve staggered nine year terms.

Elections for three panel members at a time would be held at three year intervals.

Only Senior Certified Fair Witnesses and Certified Fair Witnesses assigned to the Local Government for at least one year would be eligible to vote for Local Fair Witness Panel members.

It would not be allowed to assigned CFW or SCFW for less than two years at time to any Local Government. This will provide stability and prevent relocation for the purpose or perception of skewing a Local Fair Witness Panel election.

All SCFW assigned to the Local Government are eligible to be nominated.

A CFW assigned to the Local Government may be nominated after completing a minimum of three years of service as a CFW. If elected to a Local Fair Witness Panel, a CFW would be immediately promoted to Senior Certified

Fair Witness.

Language of Government

This is a big, big issue. It is included in this chapter because it will be in the nature of the Fair Witness to be linguistic masters.

I am definitely not a linguist. Most of you on this planet have greater language skills than I do. I am OK with that, feel a bit stupid and inferior, but hey, I accept it. Yes, I can write – in English. Obviously, that is not going to cut it for a global solution to the language barrier problem.

There are basically only three options.

1) We all learn a large number of languages and every document has multiple translations side by side.

This would fail outright as it is too difficult and impractical as there will always be translation issues to dispute. However, for at least a generation, we would have to have everything translated in the major spoken languages just to communicate. To that end, I will try to get this book translated that way.

2) The linguistic experts among us would study all the known languages and scientifically develop a new one.

3) The Korean People already did this. The Koreans are the only people in all of recorded history to accomplish this incredibly difficult feat. The government tasked their finest scholars to study the known languages and scientifically develop the Hangul alphabet and the language we

know as Korean. Not only did they accomplish this task, the government actually managed to implement it. Never been done before. Wow.

There have been spoken languages for which an alphabet or writing system was created, but that is very different and not even close in level of achievement.

Not only that, since Koreans tend to be scholarly, their technologically advanced modern society has people who have studied every major language in Human civilization on this planet.

The solution is relatively simple. We as a People recognize their contribution to Humans Being on this planet and adopt Korean as our universal language. Let them teach everyone, including myself.

For those of you who are shocked at this, think about just how difficult any other solution would be. Then realize a solution already exists. That is how I came to terms with it.

The benefit this would have to our Society is absolutely enormous.

Another practical reason to do this is it is non-political. No other existing language is as good and they all have tremendous political and cultural baggage. So not only is it an excellent solution, it is politically viable.

One potential beneficial result of adopting the only modern language on Earth is this: It may help to heal the horrible divide that exists in Korea.

Of, By and For the People

I do not speak, read or write Korean, but I am willing to learn for the benefit of all Humans Being on this planet. I have heard it spoken quite a lot. Even in my own home. It is relatively pleasant. Some languages sound like someone is hocking a lugie, no offense, but we all know that.

I have to provide a disclaimer: I was married to a Korean. If anything this makes me biased against adopting this language. But, I have to be objective and let my mind over rule my emotions. I am thinking that we all do (except of course the Koreans).

Chapter 11
Initial Setup of Government

I have given this a great deal of thought. Some of my ideas are not ready to present at the time of this writing. Others will make more sense as the old system continues to collapse. But more importantly, public discussion is required. I would like for this to be the subject of a subsequent book.

If I am still around, I could be of some assistance. Some of what is presented here is deeper than an initial read may reveal. Let these concepts sink in first.

The truth is still as stated earlier, by focusing our collective intent upon this objective goal, this future will manifest into being. Without that, our species is pretty much over. Just everyone realizing how we create the future though intent will more than justify this book.

Initially people would have to be selected to fill all the roles. Though it will take years for all the proper training and institutions to be fully and properly implemented. Some people among us are very talented at seeing a person's best aptitude and potential. They are very good at matching the best person to the given roles.

Beware that during this time of initial setup will be the most dangerous. The high level blueprint laid out in this book may be referred to again and again until things are running smoothly. The end does not justify the means.

I think what is most likely to happen is a community will be formed, away from existing cities. This governmental model will be implemented. Then it may be duplicated on a global scale.

Implementation for this proposed plan is not some pie in the sky dream floating in through the clouds. It is our last chance before we as a species are extinct on this planet. Our home is a battleground for possession. Our best chance is to liberate our living Mother from all comers who will not share and nurture her. We cannot claim ownership of her ourselves. We are caretakers of our precious home planet. I am fully aware that our planet and all the planets are living, conscious beings. Awesome beings with great power. Our Society will respect Her and She will heal and nurture us.

I cannot stress this enough, collectively, through our free will via Intent, this reality can be, will be manifest. We do not have to destroy the old order. We just have to no longer honor it and give it our power. In order to do that, my analysis of our species is, we have to have a positive image to focus our intent upon. I recommend focusing on the Rights and structures presented in this book.

Chapter 12

Economy

Well, this is the big issue isn't it? What is the ideal economic structure for the new Society. Just about everything and every type of system exists or has existed. What was good? What was bad?

I can already feel you clutching onto your hardened beliefs. You know you must be right. You are sure of it. Are you? Really? Give it up. What is your answer that you know so well to be the only correct way?

But how can that be? I am hearing so very many different answers from so many different People who are so sure they know the only way. It is like a row of different churches. Each one is believing they are the only ones who will go to Heaven. Everyone else is going the bad places. And none are living for the here and now. Hmm. How does that work?

There is nothing I can write that will please more than a few and turn off or anger the rest. Why is that? Because of attachment, mostly, and just a wee bit of manipulation. There is a quote attributed to Abraham Lincoln "You can fool some of the people all the time and you can fool all the people some of the time, but you cannot fool all the people all the time." Let us prove him correct, please.

Of, By and For the People

Look, I do not have a crystal ball. Saw one in Seoul I really want though. I am not channeling from some all knowing master. I am just a guy as intimidated by this as anyone else would be. Except for debt slavery, which we all can agree is unacceptable and the reptilian banking system which undermines entire nations for fun and profit, there is not much in common.

There is no point going into an emotional diatribe against socialism or communism or capitalism or a gift economy or barter. Because in every system you can find People who are genuinely trying to arrive at a solution. A little mutual respect is in order here.

As long as we have our Rights and genuine representative government Of the People, By the People and For the People does it really matter what form of economic system is in place? Um, yes, it matters very much.

One of the wealthiest and most powerful servants of the Vatican was Mayer Amschel Rothschild (1744 – 1812). The Godfather of the Rothschild Banking Cartel is quoted as saying: "Give me control of a nation's money and I care not who makes the laws."

And again with Baron Nathan Mayer Rothschild (1777 – 1836) He was a City of London financier, one of the major players for the international Rothschild banking dynasty. He is quoted as saying: "I care not what puppet is placed on the throne of England to rule the Empire, ... The man that controls Britain's money supply controls the British Empire. And I control the money supply."

Of, By and For the People

These guys apparently really knew what they were talking about. So first and foremost, only a legitimate representative government Of, By and For the People may be allowed to control the currency in our Society.

"The Creature from Jekyll Island" by G. Edward Griffin will help explain how the banking system came to be the way it is. Thanks also to quotes.liberty-tree.ca. The late Eustace Clarence Mullins, Jr. wrote "The Secrets of the Federal Reserve" and other works which are very relevant to this subject. I actually had the honor of hearing him speak at a Citizens for Legitimate Government meeting in Minneapolis.

I strongly recommend the documentary "The Secret of Oz". My take away from that award winning documentary is that a nation may print fiat currency without debt or interest.

As long as new currency created each year does not exceed the growth in the economy, the currency will not experience inflation. Some consider this growth to be measured in Gross National Product but that is a flawed metric in my opinion, more to it than that. As long as too much currency is not removed from circulation, there will not be economic collapse or recession and depression.

Proper management of the currency supply should result in a stabilized economy. The boom and bust cycles we have today are manufactured scientifically by the banking cabal based in the City, in London largely through manipulation of the money supply.

Of, By and For the People

This is a break from Gold or other commodity backed currency. The problem with commodity backed currency is someone already owns or controls all the potential commodities which could be used to back a currency. So it would be the same game as we have now which is gross in-equality and a tiered class structure. That is just more of the same, unacceptable.

There is a concept that money or currency itself is the problem and a system should be developed to eliminate it all together. This may be quite valid and should be studied further. Maybe, in the future, we can do away with money altogether. I recommend that all the systems outlined in this book be put in place first. Then when there is stability, the People may study the problem further and consider getting rid of currency as a relic of the past, if that is determined to be the best course of action.

For now though, it would be nearly impossible to pull that off. Some of you just laughed because you consider this whole plan impossible to pull off. Well, the joke is on you then, because if this plan is not implemented, or something very close like it, you and all that you know will die as well as our entire species. The Trans-Humanist Agenda is very real and has to be destroyed. This plan can do that.

Let me take a moment to impart the seriousness of the situation we are in. Our planet is effectively quarantined. We are isolated. If help was going to come, it would have been here by now. We are on our own, cut off. The bad guys are winning. There is simply no more time. It is up to us, trapped here on this planet to take matters into our own hands and implement this plan. I have studied for many years. I know too much about the dangers we face. But there are scant few documents which outline real paths to our own social liberation as a People.

One of the options for a decentralized currency that has wide appeal is BitCoin. It may be viable but for one thing, quantum computing and artificial intelligence. BitCoin can help us transition, but ultimately it is a temporary solution due to its inherent vulnerability. Its main flaw is the way new BitCoins are mined or created and the difficulty of protecting the primary transaction severs from hack by the spook community serving the Empire of the City.

Know that artificial intelligence and/or actual consciousness combined with quantum computing is exceedingly powerful. As long as BitCoin or any currency is digital and connected to these powerful systems, whether by Internet or electromagnetic waves, it is completely vulnerable and cannot be secure.

Our society will create and issue one standard currency for the entire planet. Protecting BitCoin and any new currency is a matter of Global Security.

Everyone I have discussed this issue with is locked into a false paradigm regarding money, commerce and economic systems. The problem is we live with a pathetically high artificial cost of living. Now, I know for a fact that we can burn salt water when exposed to a radio frequency generator transmitting at a resonant frequency of the element

Gold or Au. I also know that there are proven, simple, low cost methods to generate electricity from the air, lakes, rivers and wave motion on the coastlines. Then there is just plain separating water into hydrogen and oxygen at 15,000 cycles per second, producing more energy than can be used in a car for instance. There is more I could tell you, much more, but is outside the scope of this book.

Imagine you can run your car on tap water with relatively minor modifications. It has already been accomplished. Imagine what impact air travel, ocean shipping and trucking with minimal fuel costs will have on cost of living? What if your home used geothermal as is perfected in Norway? What if buildings were built for passive energy efficiency, minimal maintenance and made to last for centuries? How much lower would our cost of living be? Now add the fact of no tax on labor or services rendered? No interest payment on a loan only a one time fee? No more compound interest on loans of any kind, like on your dream home?

This could be our reality. The criminal cabal that plays global secret government today tries so hard to keep We the People ignorant of the truth. Their game is total abject subjugation, manipulation and control. Our game is liberation and freedom. Let the light shine in us all.

The other problem is the constant pounding out that there are too many people and not enough food or resources. I am here to tell those who do not already know, this is a lie. Plain and simple, a big lie!

Of, By and For the People

The entire population of this planet can fit in a nation the size of Texas. Most all of the use of this planet's precious resources is wasted after a single use. Thrown out, buried in landfills or dumped into the sea or burned. Most of the energy and resources go to creating massive military machines and spying on and enslaving we the People. If that energy and effort went toward ensuring everyone's basic needs are met, we would all live like kings and queens with resources to spare and not even damage our precious home planet.

Just a simple example, amazing and sometimes wonderful products can be manufactured from crude oil. A dirty, relatively expensive and more importantly, limited resource. Millions of People already know that everything made from crude oil can be made from just one of the five basic products of the hemp plant. But because hemp resin is a more complex and non-toxic substance, more stuff can be made from it. Stuff like bio-degradable plastics or methanol which burns clean in a standard combustion engine with a change to carburation settings and some gaskets. And it grows in all geographical areas of the planet without herbicides, pesticides or fertilizer. It is also a renewable resource. Unlike using food crops like corn to produce methanol, using hemp or cannabis does not keep the grain of that crop from the food supply and it would reduce the cost of that food, not increase it like it does with corn.

The cannabis plant produces fiber, fuels, medicine, paper products, building materials, and is the only plant on Earth whose grain is a complete protein for us Humans

Being. Now do you see why it is so suppressed world wide? It is also the least toxic substance known to our species, the best soil stabilization medium (its roots are hemp fiber). Since we got to this point of failure in our civilization by malevolent mind control techniques, it is good to know that consumption of the flower of the female plant is the best antidote to mind control by outside forces.

Are things looking a little less scarce and hungry now? I have not even begun to address this. This is just one of very many solutions which can be implemented with a Legitimate government Of, By and For the People at little or no cost in a matter of months, not decades. While even cleaner solutions are developed and implemented.

What about the high cost of your meds or your expensive cancer treatment? It is all fraud upon fraud. Why do you think cannabis for medicinal use is grudgingly allowed? Because the criminal cabal knows full well they cannot hide the fact it is the best known medicine, cancer treatment and nervous system protector on the planet and they impose massive taxes on its use.

But they still do not want you to know that without even trying, burning hemp instead of coal reduces costs and emission by 90%. That is an immediate short term solution and can be implemented while cleaner energy sources are produced. The Grid is killing us and other life we share this planet with. It needs to be destroyed, so do not go thinking in the old way. Remember, millions of independent, unconnected power sources are the way to go.

Of, By and For the People

The truth about the medical industry is there are many suppressed, mostly simple cures, of all known disease. And these are caused by malnutrition, air pollution, radiation poisoning, pesticides, herbicides, fertilizer runoff, chemtrails, wheat, electromagnetic radiation, synthetic drugs from big pharma and other completely artificial, unnatural causes which will be stopped.

Let the brilliant healers among us work without the restrictions that are placed on them today. In every other industry costs go down and quality goes up as new technology is developed. Old healing technology still exists from Chinese and Native American medicine much of which have not been improved upon.

It it the criminal governments that artificially drive up the cost of healing, after it makes us sick. This is not natural. Doctor Royal Raymond Rife, the Tesla of the medical industry, was sued and bankrupted by the American Medical Association. After inventing his frequency generator, he proceeded to cure all known diseases. The reasoning of the AMA was that they would not have the control and profit they wanted. See, once diagnosed, all a patient had to do was be exposed to the Rife Generator for 15 minutes and day, a few times a week, along with other doctor recommendations like drinking water, rest, and such.

How many of you know about this? Well this is a pretty informed audience or you would not be reading this book. But still, it is suppressed information. Many millions have suffered and died untimely deaths from diseases which had been cured since the 1930's have they not?

That is just one of many such technological developments in the medical industry which are suppressed which I am aware of. What about all the stuff I have not even heard or read of? Gotta be a lot of that.

There is a *lot more* I could tell you, but it is outside the scope of this book. Point being dramatically reducing the cost of living and lack of scarcity.

Anyone can have cleanly produced electricity for basically the cost of installation of a system in every home, craft and building.

Oh, it gets better, implementing clean, independent energy technology results not just in a much higher standard of living, true location independence, almost free travel and all, but it creates massive economic stimulation.

The problem is, the coal industry will have limited use. The logging industry will only be used for wood, the nuclear industry would be shut down completely, etc. Basically, it will mean massive transition.

Not to worry. In our Society with debt free, interest free currency creation, every Person will receive a steady income from the legitimate representative government.

If you did not have an electric bill, or fuel costs, no income tax, no interest on your new home, no property tax, no death taxation, dramatically reduced cost for better medical care, but you rarely got sick, how much money would you need to meet your basic needs?

I am not going to spout a number without detailed research, but I am sure it would be less than a tenth of what is needed or desired today. There is more, if you have a stipend from the government for the rest of your life, when you work or run a small shop or studio, you do not have to get paid very much because it is above your cost of living. It is all extra. This further reduces the cost of living.

Today, if you want to do something with your life, but it takes time, years maybe, that is quite difficult or practically impossible. With this system you will be able to.

Most of the jobs today are a total waste or harmful to society or for the big war and death machine or are cleaning up the messes that will mostly stop being made or are unnecessary or no longer necessary government jobs. Add improvements in efficiency and automation. I suspect that we can achieve a situation where every adult member of our Society only has to be assigned work just 15% of the time. Would you be willing for every adult to receive a paycheck for life and only have to work 15% of the time? What I mean is a normal work week, but required work assigned only three years out of twenty, after you turn 20, for instance. These are the basic infrastructure jobs.

This frees up the government to only have to deal with major medical emergencies. As suppressed cures are made available and most of the causes of what makes people sick in the first place are eliminated (cause they are criminal) the government does not have to be very big and yet it can pay for the major and emergency medical costs for every citizen at a tiny fraction of the cost today.

I am proposing all basic infrastructure be socialized, that is not for profit and managed by the people who use the services. That is the 15% of the available workforce who would rotate though these jobs during a specified age range in their lives.

Under these circumstances, an organization may reduce their cost of operations to a fraction of what it is today in terms of payroll. You could make $5 and hour, and it would be the same effect of making $50 an hour. Look at a typical paycheck today in any modern country, don't forget the extra taxes the employer has to take out of your pay that does not even show up on your paycheck. Up to 50% or more is taxes. That would be eliminated because tax on labor or services is involuntary servitude otherwise known as slavery. Everything your business needs would cost less too.

There will be no more stock exchanges or financial investment companies as we know them now. Banks will be simple banks providing basic services. Their staff will be paid like everyone else. There will be no more interest bearing loans or portfolios. Currency will be used solely for a medium of exchange until money itself is no longer even necessary.

Accumulation of currency will simply not be allowed. A cap will be set on a maximum amount of savings. What that cap is, I cannot say. But it has to happen. The maximum wealth of any individual cannot exceed a specified ratio from the minimum wealth of any individual. Excessive earning would be distributed into the system to raise the lowest level of wealth, in order to raise the highest.

Gambling will still exist, but on a much smaller scale and borrowing will not be allowed for betting.

With one currency, no ownership of land or other natural resources, a cap on accumulation of wealth, it will not be so easy to hide ill gotten gains.

Are you with me on this? Let the government cover infrastructure and basic needs for all, pay a stipend to everyone to meet their basic needs and not have millions of government employees, no debt or interest on debt.

Now, this will not stop people from wanting to provide arts, services, make stuff, build stuff, etc. When a corporation or even a non-profit organization is created today, it is a legal fiction by definition. The rules are set by the legislature.

The idea of a corporation existing for the sole purpose of making money for the shareholders is outright criminal and against the best interest of all of the People. This will not be allowed.

Organizational structures can be well defined and chartered. Unbridled, unregulated organizations become detrimental to us all. Too much regulation stemming from laws is not a good answer. The solution is in the limited definition of the chartered organization and its rules of operation. These structures are defined by a representative legislature.

Rules for businesses and other chartered organizations:

Of, By and For the People

Profits will be capped at specific amounts or percentages, excesses would be paid back to the public treasury. Pricing would be adjusted to re-balance the equation.

The defined organization structure would provide for every employee to vote for representation on the Board of Directors. And vote directly for who fills management roles at various levels of organization structure.

Today, the powers that want to be, want you to think only unions of workers who can extort more money from the owner class is the answer. This is total crap. First, there will not be an owner class anymore. Second, a properly structured organization will not have division between management and worker. Third, the members of an organization will have real power to ensure fairness in pay, safe working conditions, merit based promotion and totally open books.

After costs and pay, profits will be distributed to each functional member of the organization by formula. These rules will be set by the representative legislature. That way everyone has a vested interest in the success of their work.

The ratio between the lowest paid job and the highest paid job will be set by the legislature for everyone and every business. I am suggesting it absolutely not exceed a 7 to 1 ratio. That if the janitor makes 5 currency units, then the senior most manager could not make more than 35 units of currency, for example. What that ratio is needs to be discussed and set by the People. Then applied to all equally. What we have now is winner take all, screw everyone else. This is no longer going to be allowed.

The object is general equality. Keep in mind that senior pay position may be available to everyone. It would be merit and skill based. It may take many years to earn such a role. But if even this results in social injustice, it can and will be addressed again, and again as needed. This object is to provide incentives for encouragement and motivation. This only works if the higher paying roles are potentially achievable by anyone if they apply themselves.

All natural resources, such as minerals and fresh water are owned by the entire global community. I am with the native Peoples of America and tribes throughout this planet. They believed it not just ridiculous, but an unthinkable violation of our Mother Earth to own land or air or water. Today in many places, if you collect rain water, that is a crime. Why? Because the octopus of 140 private corporations controlled by the people who call themselves the Elite or Illuminati, the Illumined Ones, have contracts of ownership of almost all the water rights on this planet.

Fabulous monopolies have been artificially created by the same inter-bred and in-bred families over and over by using military force to seize mineral resources and the like.

International Commercial Court law is to be abolished. I am talking about the complete abolition of all existing contracts. All of them. Every corporation, every Title and Deed. Every Treaty. Every Stock and Bond. Every city charter. Most are made through fraud and deceit for the purpose of enslaving all of us. The powers they were created under will no longer exist. You, like me, will no longer recognize these fictions. None are legitimate anymore. Their day has passed. It has ended in abject failure. Resistance of the collective will of the People is futile. We stick to our Rights of the People, they cling to their draconian ways, unto their deaths. We are billions, they are thousands.

A process of transition needs to be established to restructure existing organizations as determined by law. Models will be created. Proposals based on these structural templates could be approved by the Legislature and implemented by the Executive branch.

If the chartered organization provides a basic service using natural resources, those resources are owned collectively by all the People. Not the local People or the Local Area Government, Not the Global Government either. That would be bad and an incredibly corrupting influence. The Local Government Area are entrusted as caretakers of the natural resources, not owners them.

That puts the power in the hands of the People. Organizations which mine copper, for instance, would be chartered by the Local Area Government under authority of the People. Remember, all chartered organizations are a legal fiction, a creation of the state so to speak. That means their structure is defined. These structures are open to public input and debate. All charters may be made renewable that is have a sunset clause.

Of, By and For the People

The basic concepts outlined here for the principles of our new economy combined with the governmental structures are realistic and would work in practice. It is up to the People through their representatives to work out the details.

Chapter 13
Social Institutions

When there is a social need to be met, do not think of a governmental solution first. It should be a last resort when nothing else works. I suggest the establishment of independent Social Institutions. A public educational system is such and institution. How it is designed and operated is very important. It may be funded by currency creation. It has to be chartered by representative government, but needs to operate autonomously.

I propose the creation of centers of healing using the same structural rules.

Port Facilities, Transportation Hubs, Public Stadiums, Other Sports and Arts Facilities and similar organizations may be created. These provide public services and are social institutions which can and should exist outside of the direct administration of the executive branch of government. The People, through their representative government would define clear parameters for such social institutions.

In each case, I recommend a balance of power in the managing board between the People who fill the roles and the People served. Generally a ratio of 40% of the elected members of the governing board be elected by the People who work in that organization and 60% elected by the People served by that organization.

Of, By and For the People

One basic distinction between a Social Institution and say an organization which produces widgets is the cost to the People. Social Institutions should not have a fee for their use, but would be part of the socialized financial structure and funded by money creation.

Organizations that produce goods or services which have a fee for acquisition or use would be chartered organizations, but once setup, would be funded by the revenue stream from the "sale" of their goods or service.

Another basic distinction is whether it is a vital basic need or public service, such as a healing center or transportation facility or not. A skateboard is not a vital need for every member of society, but a want for some.

In the case of protecting a child and intervention in a family unit a social institution is much desired over government intervention. This is discussed earlier. I suggest that for every 20,000 or so People within a community, a small council of elders be assembled. These groups would be looked to for guidance and wisdom. They would create a safe haven for children who are in danger. They may have other social roles as well. The intent is for the healing of all parties concerned. This is to avoid a court situation or involvement of police. When that happens, the social institutions have failed or the problem is just too big.

Does this make sense? This is a new paradigm, a different pattern to take in. I do not want to elaborate too much. This seed of thought needs to take root and grow first. Just give it some thought.

Chapter 14
Food Production

The basis of any living system for us Humans Being is clean food, water, air and soil.

In today's world, the soil of the fields are poisoned, the water and air are poisoned and after all that, the food is poisoned with chemical additives. But beyond all the physical chemical toxins created by the millions of kilograms and distributed world wide, is the spiritual poison of factory farms. In addition to all these crimes against humanity, diseased animals are fed to us. But even all these atrocities do not compare to Genetically Modified Organisms created and the passed off as food. This is a total act of war. GMO as food is a multi-generational genetic toxin designed to modify our DNA, dumb us down and also kill our species. This is not accidental, it is planned decades in advance and implemented with full intent. There is no excuse or accident involved.

This will have to stop. Completely. All use of synthetic chemical herbicides, pesticides and even most fertilizer must be banned immediately. All GMO crops need to be burned and the factories which create them destroyed.

For those of you who are still only exposed to the lies, look it up. Everyone needs to watch "Genetic Roulette – The Gamble of Our Lives". There are some very excellent sources of real information on the subject of GMO.

Of, By and For the People

The living conditions of farm animals in some factory farms and slaughtering factories are an abomination to life. There is no excuse. These facilities must be destroyed and the practice stopped completely. There is no other way. The karmic stain on our species for these crimes is enormous. We are being poisoned spiritually. It is not enough to stop eating the meat products from these sickening places. This affects our entire species. Myself included, everyone. Hundreds of millions, maybe billions of cattle, chickens, turkeys, hogs and who knows how many more types of animals are bred, grown and slaughtered in conditions which result in a cry for justice and a black stain on our collective souls. I recommend "Slaughterhouse" by Gail A. Eisnitz for a primer.

Massive scale mono-cropping has to end altogether. The problems inherent in this process are too many to go into within the scope of this book. Point is, it is not a method which results in a stable or safe system of food production. Even if it were done organically.

Only heirloom crops will be used in our Society. There is nothing new to learn. Masters of how to do it the right way abound around this planet.

Large scale corporate farms act as another tentacle of the octopus to meet out death and our own destruction.

Organic farmers will not have to deal with arrest for providing whole, unpasteurized milk for instance.

The Codex Alimentarius is an act of war against all Humans Being. This will not be allowed anymore.

Best practices will be advanced. Shared information and technology will teach People who work the land to raise food. All farmers and gardeners will have access to courses and other sources of information and products which will end these atrocities before it is too late for our species.

The existing stocks of the toxic chemicals, GMO seeds, most hybrids and poison crops will be destroyed. The scale of raising farm animals will change to a healthy manageable level. This goes for aquatic farming of too.

There will be no more dumping of raw sewage into rivers and oceans.

Our new representative governing bodies will have the authority to apportion the use of land for agriculture and other forms of farming. These will be treated as shared resources much like mineral or water resources. By eliminating the negatives, the known good methods will flourish. Farmers will not have to fear bankruptcy and be able to focus on their nurturing relationship with the land. I believe enough People will have the desire to be close to the Earth and want to live and work on farms. Proper incentives will also be put in place as necessary.

There will be many and large scale indoor farming facilities as well.

Agriculture, aquaculture and animal management technologies, tools and infrastructure will be developed and implemented in harmony with the natural order and shared freely.

The technology exists to turn sand deserts into lush, green vegetation. Weather modification technology can be used to provide proper rainfall in dry areas of the planet.

Popper management of ocean resources will allow their restoration and cleanup to levels known two hundred years ago.

Known and often suppressed solutions exist to dramatically improve the quality, quantity and cost of food production on a global scale. These can be made available and implemented.

No matter what improvements in technology are made, the underlying theme necessary is respect for life.

Chapter 15
Technology Development

This chapter is to address one of the more glaring errors of the current messed up situation of the Human civilization on this planet. The way new technology is developed and implemented or not in the current era is about as fraudulent and against the best interest of the People as it can be.

In our new yet to be name Society, new development will not be done in secret. There will be open exchange of research data. Financial gain past a modest point will be eliminated as a source of greed motivation. The People who do invent usually do not get credit for it or any financial gain much of the time anyway. But if the technology is good, like clean, cheap ways to access the energy in our environment, the inventor is often murdered and their work stolen, their labs destroyed.

I know first hand of a company in Saint Paul, Minnesota which developed technology to dramatically improve mileage and corresponding reduction in polluting emissions in existing gasoline engines. They offered modification to standard cars and trucks. The lead inventor was simply murdered. The survivors were "told" they could continue but were not allowed to exceed 70 miles per gallon. Basically they were given limits on efficiency or be killed. The was done with impunity. The state authorities were apparently powerless to do anything about it or be killed themselves.

There are hundreds of stories like this.

This is an act of treason against all life on this planet. This is not just a crime, but a very high crime deserving severe punishment. I am not supporting execution, but whatever our Society decides is the greatest punishment which is not cruel and unusual, that shall be applied. There is nothing I hate more than suppression of beneficial technology. It is just the way I am. I want peace but this crime is worthy of war.

Money and resources wasted on competing duplicate research and the billions spent by criminal corporate enterprises and illegitimate government to suppress technology is responsible for our impoverished state and much of the rape of this planet. If you think you are not impoverished by this you are unaware just how badly you have been damaged.

Medical technology has no excuse to be suppressed. Teleportation, time travel, energy devices, planetary colonization, terra-forming of planets, mining in space, construction in space the whole secret space program. How much do you lean in school about this?

Is it because you are too stupid to be told? Not likely. Is it because you would be so shocked you would die? Not likely either. Is it because some sick pieces of shit think they are gods and we are just dirty slaves? Ding! Ding! Ding! That is correct. What did you win? Access to real science and knowledge of the universe and ourselves.

Of, By and For the People

Every thought, every act you have made in your lifetime is and has been monitored. The human brain is a bio-computer. We have been hacked. The white hats who are behind some of the disclosures made by Mr. Snowden have only told us what I and many others have known or suspected since our youth. And it is only the tip of the giant iceberg. Typically, only 10% of an iceberg is above the waterline.

The malevolent beings behind this technological spying need technology to do this. Any Human has the inherent ability to see almost everything about anybody just through seeing their aura. Our brains are transmitters and receivers. Even I with limited psychic abilities can read minds if I have to. Millions of People on the planet are far ahead of me.

Every act, every thought is recorded in the Akash as we spin though space/time. This is essentially the underlying fabric of space/time. We and others can see events from the past by viewing what is called the Akashic Record. I am completely convinced of this and have a crude under-standing of how it works. Don't fret too much with all the spying, just live your life and act to generate the energies you wish to anyway. The bigger problem is the many ways technology is used against us.

Do not think of technology as just material applied sci-ence. There is technology of the mind too. I believe this is the key to our protection and especially communication. Mental applied science is very real and can be taught and learned like any other science.

Of, By and For the People

We have been given a most amazing gift by our Creator. We can create with our mind. Imagination is far more powerful than has been given credit. The main reason these technologies are suppressed or simply not taught has to do with the level of spiritual advancement of an individual. By actualizing the Rights of the People in each of our lives, I believe, that level of spiritual advancement is achieved.

This will open the door for all manner of advances in physical and mental technology development and implementation. It is true that with great power comes great responsibility. That is the course we are on.

Chapter 16
Military

Our society cannot avoid the fact it needs a military force.

I served a tour in the US Navy back in the early 1980's. I know many people who have served in one branch or another. Some from other countries as well. I did not, could not, have really known what I getting into. But, with some luck, good fortune and good shipmates, I made it through and got an Honorable Discharge. Jokes abound for these silly terms.

It takes courage to sign up and put ones life on the line to defend their country and such. It takes inner strength to follow orders. The leadership was mostly excellent though.

My job was Yeoman. Worked in Ship's Office. Dealt mostly with officers. Got to see the ship and the Navy from an administrative perspective. Got to learn something about organizational structure. A ship is very much a self contained community.

For some, there is apprehension and misunderstanding about the whole military thing. The military is and should be separate from civil government. Most people who serve their country's military are idealistic, dedicated, hard working, adventurous people. At least when they first go in. The rank and file is representative of the nation as a whole. If there is *any* hope of restoring a Constitutional Republic, it will come from veterans and active duty men and women. But I would hope to have made my point and they join the new Society instead.

The top brass is a different story. It becomes more political, that is less merit based, past a certain point. At least it seems to be that way.

I only mention my background because those who have been in the military are more likely to consider opinion and recommendation regarding military structure from someone with relevant experience.

I admire the brave men who refused the draft during the illegal Vietnam War. But I do not feel the opposite for those who joined willingly. Hey, nobody knows what they are getting into when they join. Sometimes, in youth, people do what they are told and ask questions later. They may get some seriously messed up answers to those questions, but there is a certain amount of humility in that behavior.

Veterans for Peace really know what is going on. Society at large needs to listen to what these brave people have to say.

In the model community I am presenting with this book, a military structure would look like this:

An All Volunteer Force

This is for two reasons. First you get the best people for the job, who are ready, willing and able. Second, it is just wrong to force someone to serve in the military. Encourage and suggest yes, force or compel, no.

Single Order of Rank

I really think it important to break from the two tiered model. For the most part, privilege, family connections and even wealth play too much of a role in whether a person goes in as an officer or enlisted. Experience has shown that a separate 'Class' of officers are much more likely to send the enlisted ranks to their deaths without the considerations and planning they would make for themselves. This is reflected in many aspects.

The best military will be based more on merit and respect from their peers for seniority. There are many roles, requiring many different talents and skill sets. Matching raw talent and skill to the most appropriate role is the best way to maximize training and effectiveness. This would also provide greater incentive to study and be more professional in their role.

It would also be a more accurate reflection of society. Our society would not allow dual classes.

One Branch of the Military

This is not as crazy as it might first seem. There is a tremendous amount of waste, redundancy and inter-service competition and conflict. The Army has a fleet of ships and aircraft. The Navy has more aircraft than the Air Force. The Marine corps only exists as a separate Army for the Navy for political reasons.

Not every use of force is a war. If our Society is unwilling to use force when necessary to defend itself it simply will not and cannot exist at all or for very long. Readiness and fast reaction has probably prevented wars from happening over the centuries. The People would need to define rules governing authority for a limited response to an immediate threat before an elected body can meet to review the situation.

It will be much easier to control a single military than several.

There will still be the various specializations and types of service within this organization. The costs and administrative overhead will be a fraction of what they would be with multiple, competing branches.

Improved communications and weapons security, use of cross-purpose technology, sharing of research and development, etc. It all leads to a more efficient, effective and survivable force.

Simplified Rank Structure.

Any military has to have a rank structure to be able to operate. I see three basic factors. One, is the primary role or job specification. Two, seniority within that role. Three, coordination and management across specialization.

Like any job, there is teaching and training which takes time and usually has to be learned with increasing levels of difficulty. A person has to learn and master the entry level stuff before they are ready to acquire the next, usually more complex level of knowledge and skill, etc.

No mater how much a person learns, in a group, there will be a gradient of skill levels. This is true in many aspects of civilization. Leadership is a skill and you want to select the best leaders.

I propose 12 levels of Rank or Seniority. Basically six Tiers, each with two Ranks.

Tier 1 Ranks 1 & 2:

All new members going through various stages of training and early years of experience. Similar to the first four enlisted ranks of today.

Tier 2 Rank 3 & 4:

Mid level leadership, perform their roles well. Similar to enlisted ranks 5 and 6 of today.

Tier 3 Rank 5 & 6:

Senior leadership, accomplished experts in their roles. Similar to senior enlisted ranks of Staff Sargent and above (army) / Chief and above (navy) and Warrant Officers.

Tier 4 Rank 7 & 8:

Senior leadership across specialized roles. Similar to, but more advanced than junior officer ranks today, in level of responsibility.

Tier 5 Rank 9 & 10:

High level leadership in strategic roles. Similar to commanders, army Colonels, navy Captains. High levels of responsibility.

Tier 6 Ranks 11 & 12:

Top levels. Similar to Admirals / Generals today.

Representative Leadership

The military would define its own organizational unit structures, roles and responsibilities.

Each functioning unit would vote to select its leader from the its ranks within each organization unit level.

Promotion would be merit based with clearly defined expectations.

The idea of groupings of two is they would have similar roles, but the two levels would reflect accomplishment and seniority within those roles.

The numbers of People within the Tiers would drop significantly with very few in Tier 6.

Secrecy

The military has a legitimate need for communications and operational security. The attack on New York and the bombs that killed 39 of 40 Naval Intelligence Officers who were investigating massive fraud of three trillion dollars unaccounted for could not have happened without compartmentalization of Secrecy. Essentially an entirely separate and parallel chain of command was created.

This extreme high treason happened partially due to structural gaping holes in compartmentalized secrecy. There were not proper checks or oversight even within the Pentagon which would have prevented the attacks on the eleventh of September, 2001.

Of, By and For the People

This issue is not that simple. It is a fine line between too many people knowing an operational plan and not enough qualified military personnel being informed. However, what goes on today with secrecy is treason against the People of Earth plain and simple. I am convinced that most use of secrecy in the military and government today is to hide crimes against the People.

It is clear that the security system failed long before that day. Inexcusable abject failure in fact. How can this be prevented from ever happening in the future, an attack on our own Society from a criminal element within the military? And subsequent cover-up?

A serious open debate needs to take place in order to define rules for the military in our Society. Rules which would be more effective from a security standpoint and from a checks and balances standpoint. Individuals in our Society who have skills and relevant experience need to weigh in and be heard.

It is my understanding from listening to whistle blower testimony that there are other issues as well. Such as a ridiculous amount of redundancy to the tune of billions or even trillions of dollar in waste just from concurrent duplicate secret projects where information is not shared.

In the former united States, true civilian government oversight and ultimately control simply did not exist. Presidents, Senators even members of the Joint Chiefs of Staff had been routinely denied access to locations and information. How is that? This sort of treason cannot be allowed in our Society.

Today, secrecy is used to suppress technology to the determent of the People. This technology is rightfully owned by the People. Energy, medical, materials, bio-engineering and nano technology which could be put to good use and are not. To me, this is nothing short of High Treason against all the Humans Being on the planet. It is even worse in that select individuals do have access to these technologies. What we have now is a tier 1 science which is secret and a tier 2 science which is known to be false or limited, taught in the colleges and universities.

What this did was create a completely separate civilization which is essentially at war with the vast majority of the People. They are trying to create a total Master / Slave society with nothing in between. The sociopaths want to play god over everyone else.

One suggestion I will make is if anyone in the military refuses proper access or to provide proper information to civilian government authority be arrested and charged with treason or whatever is appropriate. If found to be a valid charge, they could be demoted to the lowest rank, kicked out of the military and then face whatever the People through the proper legislation, deem. But, as taught to me by a Navy Chief who I served under, there are *always* two sides to every story. That is why there must be public hearings and courts. Accused and convicted individuals still have Rights which must be respected.

One argument for military personnel refusing to answer to a person in the role of proper civilian authority is they may know that the individual is a traitor or loyal to a foreign power. In the present circumstance, this has often been the case. That does not by itself account for the incredibly criminal system that exists today.

The model I am proposing can help to prevent this from happening again. However, input is needed by people well versed in these issues who can make good recommendations that may be implemented.

Individuals who report criminal or questionable acts by members of the military to the civilian government need to be protected.

The need to know thing has just gotten out of control. There is not only Need to Know, but Right to Know and Duty to Inform.

And finally, have fewer levels of secrecy with oversight structures in place at each level.

If this matter is not properly resolved, what happened already could happen again, even our new Society. Do Not Allow That To Happen.

Military Intelligence

This will be the only governmental intelligence organization. It will be responsible for all manner of intelligence collection and analysis relative to the defense of our Society and the planet. It is primarily about information collection and analysis, not operational roles which are to be conducted by other military personnel.

It will provide briefs and consultation to the Executive and Legislative branches of civilian government.

Its primary role is to aid in planning and execution of military operations.

Its duties include anticipation of risk and threat from all civilizations other than ours and our space environment. This role includes asteroid tracking to avoid collision.

Track all objects orbiting the planet and any other planet where we have operations or civilian communities. This includes tracking of objects which may collide with the planet and need to be diverted or destroyed.

It will have authority to monitor communications and movements of other civilizations for threat analysis.

It is not to be allowed to monitor or spy on our civilian government or citizens. They may assist law enforcement as per legislation.

Civilian Control

The top leadership position would be selected from within the 12th rank, by the First Executive and approved by the Global Senate. The office would be re-appointed every three years. It could be the same person if appropriate.

The Global First Executive and Senate will have authority to remove from office any member of the military for cause.

The Global Legislature may designate military service awards and medals and set objective criteria for their achievement. The Global First Executive may assign awards and medals by decree. The Senate and House of Representatives may assign awards and medals by majority vote.

Military pay and budget is subject to approval of the Global First Executive after passing the Global Senate and House of Representatives on an annual, bi-annual or tri-annual basis.

Any member of the military would have to resign or retire from the military before they could hold any office in the civilian government.

There would be no separate legal code for the military. Members would have the same rights to a trial by jury as a civilian. Jury and Judges should not be active military as this would potentially be a conflict of interest. But it may be good if they are former military for a better understand of the situation. This may not always be practical in the field, but the intent of impartiality must be maintained.

Military Duty and Responsibility

The duty of the military in this Society is to defend and protect the People and their Rights from all enemies both within and outside our Society.

The military and civilian governments will never be allowed authority to initiate a war of aggression.

Efforts will be made to provide the finest, state of the art, defensive armor, weaponry and craft. High technology defensive and offensive capability is important, but low technology is just as important to keep and maintain. Any and all new and old technologies must be evaluated for their potential application to military use or threat.

Strategic centers, resources, facilities, bases and population centers need to be protected and defended at all times. Inter-dimensional beings, nano technology weapons including sentient black goo and some forms of artificial intelligence are potentially our greatest threat. Strategies must be developed to counter every conceivable threat.

This Society is for Humans Being and we share this planet and outer space with many other civilizations of Non-Humans Being. Some are very powerful. There will also be a period of assimilation of Peoples of Earth with many outside our yet to be named Society. During our formative years, we will need military protection from old order forces who may be bent on our destruction.

The military shall not be burdened with actions better suited to civilians or civilian government.

Promotion and demotion is part of the military's managerial duty.

The military will advise law enforcement, but will not make arrests or be law enforcement. If, in some circumstance the criminal organization is essentially an army itself, then it would be appropriate for a First Executive to request Military intervention. This needs to be closely debated and when a decision is made, done under public scrutiny.

Force Structure

Military recruitment should be balanced across all local area governments.

Objective guidelines for testing, training, rank, specialization and force structure will be drawn up by military staff and submitted to the Global Legislature for approval by majority vote. The Global First Executive will sign or veto these guidelines.

Armories and bases of operation will be kept and maintained strategically across all governed areas. Stocks of weapons, armor, Earth bound and space bound vessels and craft will be kept and maintained. Operational forces will be fully staffed. Non-operational equipment will be maintained in a state of readiness to be fully staffed in time of need or war.

The military will be structured to have a minimal active duty force in time of peace, with the ability to call to active duty veterans who would assume their previous rank and role in time of need. Preparation time for up-to date training will likely be needed before assuming full responsibilities of previous rank.

History has demonstrated, that a large standing military has great potential for abuse of the Rights of the People. But a large population of trained veterans is also the best defense. It would be appropriate for a large proportion of young men and women serve a short three year term of service. These will become the base of veterans who may return to service in time of need or war while new recruitment is scaled up.

All service is voluntary. A unit may refuse an order, even in wartime. This will be minimized by units electing their own leaders. In practice, a refusal of orders would likely only happen when the majority or all of a unit is sure it is a bad order. The issue of no confidence in their leader is resolved by the units electing their leaders.

Prisoners of War

All military and civilian prisoners captured in war or defensive conflict will be the responsibility of the civilian government.

Prisoners will be introduced to our Rights and culture.

Their basic needs will be met.

They will be held captive for as short a time as possible and in as humane conditions as is reasonable.

Their culture and technology will be studied for anything useful we might want to do or use ourselves.

There will be an opportunity for them to be assimilated if appropriate.

Closure

All wars need to end.

Military forces will specifically target strategic and tactical targets. By minimizing casualties, which means death & injury, the prospects for eventual victory and peace will be increased.

The civilian government is required to come up with contingency plans for a peace settlement.

No such plan may include the removal of our Rights for any reason.

Better to fight and die free than to be enslaved again.

Chapter 17
Educational System

As a high school drop-out, some might suggest that I should not be the one to deal with this issue. They would be right, except I have seen the educational system from a different perspective and have insights those within the system do not have. I also have not been broken by the system and have no vested interest in maintaining it the way it is now.

First, start completely over from scratch. A proper examination of the best examples from different cultures and educational system would be a good move.

Second, today's education system is primarily designed to stunt the mental growth of the student. A great deal of time, money and energy has been spent figuring out how to sever a child from their natural mental talents. It is all about creating artificial limits and trying to force those limits onto the student. I suggest reading "Magical Child" by Joseph Chilton Pearce to gain insight in the natural unfolding of a child's natural abilities and intelligence.

Third, the system today is designed not only to force the student to accept limitation but to break them to accept authoritarian rule. The goal seems to be the creation of good little robot slaves who will work for the ruling class and not ask questions. If you have a problem with the truth I am clearly pointing out, well, you are either guilty of letting the system beak you, and/or, you are guilt of creating and implementing the system. Deal with it.

I want to lay out a few suggestions for the sake of discussion. Problems I have had probably affect whole groups of People.

I propose the creation of single, but large educational service institution within each Local Area Government. A central core campus with small satellite branches to meet the needs of Society. This will provide for many parallel educational institutions which would compete for performance. Best practices will develop and be shared.

The key is the people who use those services and parents of children who use this service have a vote for representation on the governing board. The Governing Board would consist of 60% / 40% representation. 60% of the seats elected by the People who use the service. 40% of the seats elected by the teachers and staff of the organization itself. Elections would be held on a standard three year election cycle.

I see three aspects of education which should be treated separately. The first is education itself, reading, writing, arithmetic and such. The second is extracurricular activities such as sports, drama, various clubs and such. The third is socialization of children growing up with others in their age group.

I found it incredibly difficult and unproductive to learning to spend a brief time on one subject, bell rings (screw your bell Pavlov), switch to another subject, deal with it just a little, bell rings, do that again with another subject. Do it again next year. That does not work for me.

I have taken several professional courses. These were most excellent. I was taught much more effectively when immersed in a particular course for a day or days at a time. That is work days, not 24 hour days. The lesson plans were awesome. The next piece of information seemed to anticipate my next question.

Everyone has a body clock. Some cultures recognize that we get burned out in the mid afternoon. I always had to fight falling asleep, even if it was my favorite class, in the mid afternoon time. These human cycles need to be accounted for.

Proper nutrition and a balance of mental and physical activity and break time will provide the student optimal learning ability. Without these much time is wasted in a child and adult student's attempt to learn and the teacher's attempt to teach.

I found that what helped me adapt and thrive in the military the most was my experience in school sports programs. The coaches I had in my youth taught valuable lessons that went far beyond playing or competing.

It is the extracurricular programs that teach culture, social and practical skills. The teachers who run such programs are like coaches. The benefits not only help throughout one's life, but can lead to careers and professional achievements. This may be especially true of the arts.

What if an educational institution had centers of learning for each subject. One that students of all ages would attend. The course level would be based on merit not age. A student might have a higher level of learning accomplishment in some subjects versus other subjects. Criteria could still be set for achievement in various subjects.

To make this work, each student would have a counselor to advise and guide them through the process over the years. These counselors would have to have some degree of independence within the system to be more effective. They would work with the student and their parents or guardian.

Sports programs are age or size dependent for fairness and more fun. But they could be conducted parallel to the courses which are not.

Other extracurricular activities would totally depend on the program. Some might want students at a similar age, others might not. But these could also be parallel to the course work part of education.

Teachers need to have much more independence to teach as they deem best for their students. This business of teaching to a standardized test is not real teaching. Standardized textbooks cannot be forced upon a teacher for optimum performance.

Standardized textbooks tend to be politically motivated and become some truth mixed with lies, some truths withheld, etc. Let those who are the teachers control their lesson plans. Time will tell and improvements can be made based on best practices like any progressive industry.

Of, By and For the People

Teaching should use methods appropriate to differing student aptitudes. People are different. Some are more visual, some are more audio or tactile. A good coach plays to the strength of their team. A good teacher can teach to optimal learning ability of their student.

You know how it is often said we only use 10% of our brain? Or that we only use a limited amount of our potential intelligence? There is much more to learn and to develop which Humans Being are capable of. I have delved into the mind and human consciousness a bit. Our educational system has to go far beyond what exists today if it is to teach to our real capability. We are not meat sacks or just physical. We are immortal mental and spiritual beings and our physical body is temporal.

The has been much effort by social engineering planning institutions like the Tavistock Institute to dumb us down to a pathetic level. They have placed professors in college who try to con their students to believe their limited five sense reality is all there is. That the chemicals in our mind and body control us when our mind and spirit control our physical body. They push the "this world is all there is'" philosophy. This insidious institution has been our enemy since its beginning. Look where it is based in the heart of the Empire of the City. Look that up.

The truth is very often the opposite to what is taught in colleges and universities today. This is by design. This will not be allowed in our educational institutions. I want to see the natural unfolding and development of our children and ourselves, not enslavement.

In the US at least, teachers are not really promoted or retained based on merit. Administrator get paid vastly disproportional to the actual teachers doing the real work. That is not in the best interest of society. The issue of unions is dealt with elsewhere in this book. It certainly appears to me that the teacher's union has had a very destructive effect on the quality of education in society. If you want an example, compare private schools to union-ized public schools.

Much of the pathetic restriction of what it is to be Human is taught and promoted in the name of religion. Stupid religious groups attack the development of knowledge. Here is an example I need to tell. As a person who has had psychic and spiritual experiences throughout my life, and especially in my childhood and youth, I know from personal experience many things which the brain dead zombies in much of the world would want to kill me for even mentioning.

Modern day psychiatry not only fails to grasp the significance of left and right brained aspects to our personality and awareness, they classify all psychic and spiritual experiences as other than what they are. They define aspects of human behavior as mental illness which need psychotropic drugs to treat. They add more to their self serving list every year! There may be some merit to their work, but the greater part is antithetical to what it is to be Human.

Tuesday Lobsang Rampa was who he said he was. That is incomprehensible to most all formally educated people.

But not to me. Not just because I recognized and rejected formal education for what it is, but because I can relate to much of his teaching from personal experience. In "The Third Eye", he tells of growing up in Lhasa, Tibet, before the Communist Chinese invaded and destroyed that spiritually advanced nation.

His teacher would take the young students to the roof of their building, high in the mountains, where they would lay down to sleep. But instead of sleeping, they would leave their physical bodies and form up as a class in their astral bodies, some would call this lucid dreaming. The Lama, their teacher would hold class this way. He took the children to different nations and cities around the Earth to teach geography. They saw all the major cities of the world and the people. Sometimes he took them to outer space to learn about the solar system. Sometimes to other planets orbiting distant stars, with civilizations to observe them.

I have experienced lucid dreams countless times. There are classes you can take, even right here in America where anyone can learn to do this. Check out the Monroe Institute or the Project Camelot interview with Doc Barham. I can tell you this stuff is real. But either you already know it or you may have a mental block against it. Yet, all this is considered mental illness by Psychiatrists! It is considered evil or whatever by many religious idiots as well.

Carlos Castenenda is also considered a fraud or his work pure fiction. But while his work may have been fictionalized, the Toltec teaching in them are very real. I know because of my own experience and subjective reality.

I can tell you, I would have been dead a long time ago if this were not the case. I have saved my life a few times with this knowledge. There is no rational explanation for how I am still in my physical body if you knew what I have been though and experienced, at least by the limited paradigm of reality taught in school and most churches.

This is not really religion or a belief system. It is just a normal part of Human nature. There are many areas of knowledge which you can prove to yourself but cannot objectively prove to others. There are inherent dangers involved in the exploration of our natural consciousness, but that is all the more reason to have good teachers.

Our educational system need to dramatically expand its limited boundaries and clean out the lies and false teachings. If you search for the source of some of the lies taught in schools and colleges today, you will find they are unfounded or have been insidiously implanted by subversive organizations. If you dig deeper, you will find the ones who made it their mission to spread the lies know the real truth.

Education needs to be open and free to people of all ages, all the time. There is so much to learn and our time in this world is so short. In order to "make it" in today's rate of new development in virtually all areas of expertise, continuing education is necessary.

In our global community, knowledge would be shared. Best practices are more valuable and advance faster with a wider pool of input.

The economics of education today is somewhat pathetic at many levels. That issue is society wide and is dealt with in another chapter.

In this scenario, teachers, coaches and those running the other extracurricular programs would be honored with the high degree of respect they deserve.

This business of children lugging backpacks full of books like pack animals has to stop.

One of the ways the united States fell into tyranny is the dumbing down of the school system and suppression of and restriction of access to knowledge.

But, it is my contention that even worse is the fact that the school structure has been authoritarian in nature from the students perspective. It seems it was all about breaking the spirit of the student in order to get them to accept an authoritarian work environment. This made it easier for authoritarian government and policies to occur. This is completely, totally wrong six ways to Sunday. I am so glad I quit when I did.

If a young man or woman goes through the system and does not see the need to defy an authoritarian system, then they become a broken shell of what they could have been.

Therefore, the schools in this new Society will teach freedom and personal responsibility. It will impart the values of a free and free thinking society in order to perpetuate those values.

Homework? Homework!!! If you got me for the whole day, do not expect me to take it home and do more. Balance in life, especially between school or work and home life is essentially to quality of life.

In fairness, looking back, I did have some good teachers and went mostly to private Catholic school. But they were like spies that slipped through the cracks. They had to work within the system that existed in the hopes the values they taught would survive. They planted the seed of thought, and it did grow. I am sure a few would approve of my overall message and passion. Some were true visionaries who wanted to cause change and create the sort of Society I am writing about in this book.

I guess if you approve of the message in this book, you have to think kindly on at least some of the teachers that produced me. I thank Sister Marybeth, from 3rd grade, you were the best! I will never forget that day. She taught her class, she loved her children, that we knew the basics. She taught us that now that we knew how to read, how to write and basic arithmetic, if we never had another day of formal schooling, we knew enough now. That if we apply ourselves and these basic skills, we could learn anything. She taught us how to think properly and to ask questions.

One day, as a child, I was walking by the Convent and met her. I was pretty sad. I had been thinking about life, and what that meant for my future and how things were just going to keep on the way they were. She stopped to talk to me. She asked me why the sadness. "Cause when

I grow up, I guess I'm just going to be a scientist and work for some big corporation like DuPont or Dow."

She paused, looked me in the eye and said "It doesn't have to be that way, if that is not what you want." It might not seem like much, but she gave me real hope that day. It was the first time the realization began that we can change our future.

Some of you might think, hey that's not such a bad gig to look forward to. It was more than that, it was thinking things would never change that got to me. This was also in the context of the Vietnam War going on. And on.

I remember geography class. Looking at Southeast Asia. I was learning about Vietnam. I told my teacher, wow, what a beautiful country, I really want to go and visit there. She gave me a quizzical look. I knew there was something she wanted to tell me but couldn't.

My sadness is nothing, even my hopes and fears are nothing when compared to the children of my generation in Vietnam. It is too late to say "Make sure that does not happen again." I has happened again, over and over now. This rule by criminal cabal and global tyranny has to end.

You who teach, the values you impart are a big part of a child's life. Sometimes you have more influence than a child's parents who trust you to teach their children well. Teach the right values. You do make a difference, one way or another.

Look for the innovators, the free thinking teachers to teach the next generation. Like what happened to me, only this time the innovators won't have one hand tied behind their back and have to work within a restrictive institution.

Chapter 18
My Vision for Humans Being

I envision that we, as a species and a soul group will unite and form a new Society which is in harmony with the natural order.

Healing technology which can preserve our lives in a healthy state for centuries, leading to near physical immortality will be available to all.

Clean energy technology will enable us to live almost anywhere and promote real wealth and wealth equality.

Transportation technology which closes distances on the planets where we live and between them will be available to everyone and little to no cost.

Anti-Gravity will be perfected to the point of holding up movable cities.

Mental and Spiritual Technology will surpass physical technology.

Humans Being will achieve ascendancy to a higher vibrational frequency have powers which enable true freedom from oppression, subjugation and control by malevolent and parasitic beings.

That Cosmic Consciousness / Samadhi will be achieved by all who turn away from service to self and serve others.

Of, By and For the People

That Humans Being will take our rightful place among inter-stellar civilizations and become guides and teachers to others throughout the Galaxies in the ocean of space.

Here is something I penned on the eve of my 18th birthday. It originally used the word His, but I really wanted a gender neutral word. Changed it to Her because the creative force seems to be feminine. It is included here because is it a description of a vision I had of all the works and constructs of our species separate from all else, seen over a vast time, condensed to a moment.

= =

Searching Through Her Endless Expressions

The Machine lay

You could see through It's complexity

It was old, rusty, torn & fixed

Always It moved, forward into time

About Its base, beings, creatures of the machine moved

There were inside also, to every place and function, others like those below

And it seemed time sped up

Faster It moved, and lo, great change was taking place inside

And there were ever from below more beings entering as those inside mysteriously left

Always there were more to come underneath

Of, By and For the People

As the Machine moved, a trail It had, tracing back to where the edges of infinity never seemed to stop

Before It, It created a path

And a wake It made, like to a ripple of waves as a pebble descends through an endless sea

It grew again presently, slowly at first, but then with the pride of a false grandeur

It learned

A Machine it seemed but with life, the life of those to the least from which It was made

It had but seemed to grow

It only changed

And at any given moment It was still

The lines of Its future were made by Its past

And it seemed, also, that It was dissolved into the space It traversed

There were those inside which wrought change

Forging strong healthy ideas, welding with their love, smoothing with their peace

Creating a magnificent image which thirst only for knowledge of God

And within the core of every being was light, and around that light darkness

Always, to see toward the light there was light

Always, to see toward the darkness there was darkness

Of, By and For the People

And there were those inside which grew fear and bred hate

And these did create a foul image

With malice it destroyed

With ignorance it prospered

Yet its design was equally intricate

And where the two met, they entwined

And the Machine was a reflection of Its creators, alone and as one

Yet poised within the ocean of space, It was always melting, dripping endlessly into the void

And rhythm could be heard, sound felt

Vibration within vibration, holding all the pebbles, all the sea, together in harmony

Accord did blend with discord

And all the sea, and all the seas did become but an expression of Her

The elusive, all pervading...

by

Angelo Patrick Arteman

aka Gerry Carton

Bibliography

Invaluable sources of information and inspiration which are referenced in or otherwise influenced this book.:

Alex Collier, Author "Defending Sacred Ground"

Bases Project, Miles Johnston, Sentient Fluid Black Goo

Bill Knell, Presenter, Presentations at Lincoln, Nebraska in 1994, exposed truths and suffered greatly

Bill Still, Created Documentary "The Secret of Oz"

Cable News Network, CNN March 30, 1981, Dr. Joseph Giordano

Carlos Casteneda, Author "Journey to Ixtlan", "Tales of Power"

Cathy O'brien & Mark Phillips, Authors "Trance-Formation of America"

Christopher Bird Author "Secrets of the Soil"

David Hatcher Childress, Author, "Anti-Gravity and the World Grid"

David Icke, Author "The Biggest Secret", "The Truth Shall Set You Free"

Dr. Raymond Bernard, Author "The Hollow Earth"

Eustace Clarence Mullins, Jr., Author "The Secrets of the Federal Reserve"

G. Edward Griffin, Author "The Creature from Jekyll Island"

Of, By and For the People

Gail A. Eisnitz, Author "Slaughterhouse"

Henrik Palmgren, RedIceCreations.com Interviews with Peter Levenda and Joseph P Farrell

Howard Zinn, "A People's History of the United States"

Imanuel Velikovsky, Author, "Mankind in Amnesia", "Earth in Upheaval"

Inelia Benz, ascension101.com

James Bamford, Author "The Puzzle Palace"

James McCanney, jmcanneyscience.com Electric Universe Theory

Joseph Chilton Pearce, Author "Magical Child"

Josh Reeves, "Lost Secrets of Ancient America volume I" and internet radio shows at www.theglobalreality.com

Kerry Cassidy, Project Camelot www.projectcamelot.com

Lao Tzu, Tao Teh Ching, Translated by John C. H. Wu

Laura M. Eisenhower - Mind Control, UFOs, ETs, New World Order, Illuminati

Marshal B. Gardner, Author "A Journey to the Earth's Interior"

Michael Cremo, Author, "Forbidden Archeology" with Richard Thompson

Michael Tsarien, Author "Irish Origins of Civilization"

Paramahansa Yogananda, Author "Autobiography of a Yogi", "The Divine Romance"

Of, By and For the People

Peter Tompkins & Christopher Bird Authors "The Secret Life of Plants"

Project Camelot: Doc Barham interview by Kerry Cassidy

Project Camelot: George Kavassilas interview by Kerry Cassidy, Resonated with me most of all her interviews

Project Camelot: Total Recall My Interview with Mark Richards

Robert A. Heinlein, Author, "Stranger in a Strange Land"

Robert A. Monroe, Author "Journeys Out of the Body"

Sovereign Mind Radio with Sonia Barrett Preston Nichols - The Music of Time, November 18, 2009

Tuesday Lobsang Rampa, Author "The Third Eye" "The Hermit" and 15 other books

William Bramley, Author "The Gods of Eden"

William Cooper, Author "Behold A Pale Horse"

Whitby Streiber, Author "Communion", "Transformation", UnknownCountry.com

Zacharia Stitchen, Author "Earth Chronicles" series